EDEXCEL

GCSE MUSIC

Revision Guide

PAUL TERRY

The author

Paul Terry

studied music at the University of East Anglia and trained as a teacher at the University of Cambridge. He taught from primary to sixth-form level for 20 years, including 15 years as head of music at a well-known public school, after which he combined examining with part-time teaching at his local university.

Paul was an examiner for the Associated Board of the Royal Schools of Music for nearly 30 years, and has been chief examiner in music for both OCSEB (now part of OCR) and Edexcel (for whom he pioneered the introduction of Music Technology as an A Level subject). He has also served as a member of the Secondary Examinations Council and its successor the Schools Examinations and Assessment Council, and has been employed as a music consultant by several examining boards.

First published 2016 in Great Britain by
Rhinegold Education
14-15 Berners Street
London W1T 3LJ, UK
www.rhinegoldeducation.co.uk

You should always check the current requirements of your examination, since these may change.

Editor:
Thomas Lydon

Cover and book design:
Fresh Lemon Australia

Edexcel GCSE Music Revision Guide
Order No. RHG308
ISBN: 978-1-78558-168-7

Exclusive Distributors:
Music Sales Ltd
Distribution Centre
Newmarket Road
Bury St Edmunds
Suffolk IP33 3YB, UK

Printed in the EU

Contents

Introduction

This book is about the GCSE Music qualification offered by Edexcel, first examined in 2018. The requirements are not the same as those for other boards offering GCSE Music. GCSE Revision Guides for other boards are available from Rhinegold Education.

Edexcel GCSE Music has three components:

1. **Performing**	Solo performance and ensemble performance	**60 marks:** 30% of your total GCSE mark
2. **Composing**	One composition to a set brief and one free composition	**60 marks:** 30% of your total GCSE mark
3. **Appraising**	Exam paper (1 hour and 45 minutes) on set works and unfamiliar music	**80 marks:** 40% of your total GCSE mark

Work for performing and composing has to be submitted by a date set by your teacher (no later than 15th May in your examination year). The Appraising paper is taken on a date set by Edexcel in the main exam period (late May to late June).

This book will help you to get a good mark in the Appraising (or 'listening') paper. The questions in this exam paper are based on extracts of music that will be played as you write your answers. Most of these extracts come from eight set works, two from each of the four areas of study, contained in the *Edexcel GCSE (9–1) Anthology of Music* (scores: ISBN 978-1-29-211838-3, recordings: ISBN 978-1-29-211839-0). There will also be two extracts of unfamiliar music that is related in some way to these set works.

This guide includes sections on each of the eight set works, notes on the elements of music to help you answer questions on unfamiliar music, tips for effective revising, and a glossary of technical terms that you need to learn.

For success in the exam **you need to know** how the music in the set works is constructed, how it creates a mood and how its composer has used such musical devices and elements as melody, rhythm, harmony, structure and so on. To do this, you need to know the *exact* meaning of the technical terms included in this book and how to use them correctly when describing music.

Important technical terms are printed in bold type, and also appear in the glossary on page 72.

For the exam **you will not need to know** the biographies of composers, or their precise dates of birth, or lists of their other works.

Make sure you listen to the set works regularly and can identify the features listed in this guide. As the exam approaches, it will help to practise timed listening papers such as those included in *Edexcel GCSE Music Listening Tests 2016* by Simon Rushby (RHG307, ISBN 978-1-785-58167-0), published by Rhinegold Education.

AREA OF STUDY 1:

Instrumental music 1700–1820

Instrumental music includes works for orchestra and works for solo instruments. This area of study focuses on the Baroque concerto and the Classical sonata.

During the **Baroque** period (1600–1750) orchestras were established and the first types of orchestral music, such as the **concerto**, appeared. The concerto is a work that features the contrast between a soloist (or small group of soloists) and an orchestra. It usually has three **movements** in the order fast–slow–fast.

If there is only one soloist the work is called a **solo concerto**. If there is a group of soloists, as in the case of the first set work, it is called a **concerto grosso** ('big concerto').

Well-known composers of the Baroque period include Purcell, Bach, Handel and Vivaldi.

During the **Classical** period (1750–1820) the piano replaced the **harpsichord** as the main keyboard instrument of the day. The piano **sonata**, along with the sonata for solo instrument (such as violin or flute) and piano, became an important type of music from this period onwards, usually written in three or four movements.

Well-known composers of the Classical period include Haydn, Mozart, Beethoven and Schubert (some of whose music looks forward to the Romantic period).

Set work 1

Bach: Brandenburg Concerto No. 5 in D major (3rd movement)

Context

This is the last movement of *'Brandenburg'* Concerto No.5, the fifth of six concerti grossi that Bach sent to the Margrave of Brandenburg in Germany in 1721, compiled from works he had already written.

They were originally intended to be played by a small court orchestra, but were probably never performed at Brandenburg and were not published until 1850, one hundred years after Bach's death.

Period and genre

Late Baroque. **Genre** means type of work: this is a **concerto grosso**.

Resources

Three solo instruments (the **concertino**): flute (*flauto*), violin (*Violino principale* or principal violin) and harpsichord (*cembalo*).

Accompaniment (the **ripieno**): a small chamber orchestra with parts for violin, viola, cello and violone (a predecessor of the double bass, marked 'contrabasso' in the Anthology score).

This concerto is the first ever to feature a solo part for harpsichord. Bach may have written this **virtuoso** part for himself to play, in order to demonstrate a new harpsichord purchased by the court where he worked.

In sections where the harpsichord is not used as a solo instrument it takes an accompanying role as part of the **basso continuo**, playing chords indicated by a **figured bass** (a process known as the **realisation** of the figured bass). The notes in a basso continuo part are also played by at least one bass instrument, such as a cello or double bass.

Structure

Ternary form (ABA):

A Bars 1–78 (0:00)	**B** Bars 79–232 (1:18)	**A** Bars 233–310 (3:49)
Fugato	Ritornello structure	Fugato
D major	B minor	D major

The A section is a **fugato** in D major. This means that it is like the opening of a **fugue** in which the opening tune (called the **subject**) is taken up by each of the other instruments in turn. Each new part enters in **imitation** of the previous part, overlapping with it, often at a higher or lower pitch.

The B section begins and ends in B minor and has a **ritornello** structure in which **episodes** based on just the first four notes of the subject alternate with **ritornelli** ('little returns') of other material from the A section.

Apart from the D-major chord at the start of bar 233, the final A section is a repeat of the opening fugato. Bach didn't write this out, but instead wrote *Da Capo* ('from the top') at the end of bar 232 to indicate that the first section should be repeated. This particular type of ternary structure is therefore often called **da capo** form.

Tonality

Tonality refers to the use of keys in a piece of music. It is nothing to do with tone.

This movement is in D major. Because almost all of the music is derived from the opening bars, Bach relies on changes of texture (see below) and key rather than on different melodies to create contrast.

The first section is in D major and includes modulations to the dominant (A major), which is the key a 5th above the tonic, D.

The middle section is in B minor (the relative minor of D major) with modulations to *its* dominant (F♯ minor) and to A major.

Melody

The entire movement is based on triadic and scalic (stepwise) ideas heard in the first few bars. The opening melody of Section B uses the first four notes of Section A, transposed up from D major to B minor:

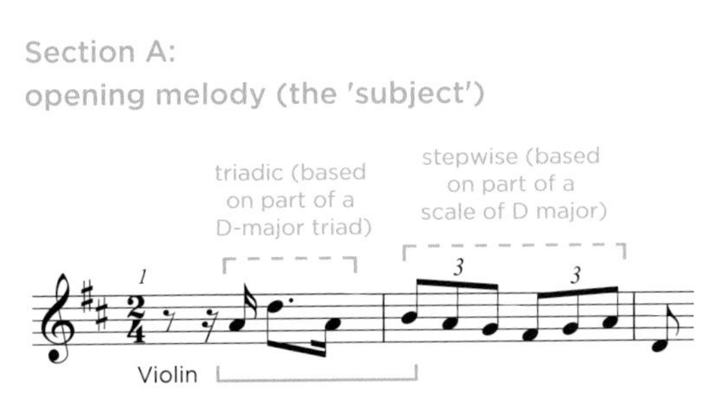

Similarly, the rippling quavers that accompany the flute at the start of Section B are derived from the pattern first heard in bar 5:

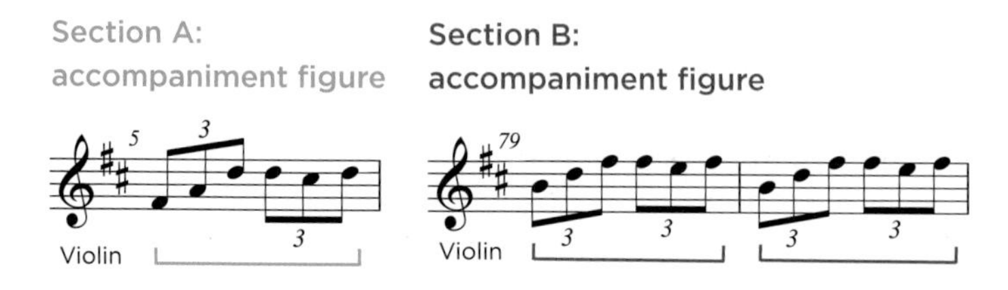

The melodic writing includes frequent use of **sequence** and two types of **ornament** - the **trill** (***tr***) and the **appoggiatura** (printed as a small note and generally played as a quaver). In accordance with convention, performers frequently add additional ornaments to match those written by Bach.

The imitative texture (see below) ensures that all instruments have some share in the melodic material.

Rhythm

- The tempo is *Allegro* (fast) and doesn't change
- The movement is written in simple duple metre ($\frac{2}{4}$) but triplet quavers make it sound like compound duple metre ($\frac{6}{8}$). In accordance with Baroque practice, the pattern ♪. 𝅘𝅥𝅯 is played as ♩ ♪ (3) to fit the triplet feel of the music
- The movement is in the style of a gigue (a fast courtly dance of the period, generally in $\frac{6}{8}$ time and related to the jig of folk dance)
- Triplets and dotted rhythms dominate, plus semiquavers in the harpsichord part.

Texture

Apart from bars 1–2 (and their repeat in 233–234) where the unaccompanied melody creates a brief monophonic texture, the movement is contrapuntal throughout, with frequent use of imitation.

The texture of Section A could also be described as a **fugato** (or as 'fugal'). It is not an actual **fugue**. A **stretto** (close imitation) starts in bar 64, just before the end of the A section.

The violone (double bass) plays in the **tutti** sections, mainly **doubling** the cello. All other parts are largely independent, although flute and solo violin sometimes double (e.g. bars 33–44) or play in parallel 3rds (e.g. 107–114).

Bach uses changes in texture to produce areas of contrast. For example, the opening four-part texture is followed by a more fully textured **tutti**, while the harpsichord solo in bars 163–176 has only a two-part canonic texture. A free canon (this time between flute and solo violin) starts in bar 193.

Dynamics

Like most Baroque composers, Bach included few dynamic markings in his scores. Instead he relied on changes in texture, such as those between soloists and full ensemble, to produce contrasts, as well as on the intuition and experience of performers.

In general, much Baroque music depends on the use of **terraced dynamics** in which there are clear shifts between loud and soft passages, without the use of gradual crescendos and diminuendos. In the Anthology score, dynamic markings printed within square brackets have been added by the book's modern editor rather than by Bach.

Harmony

- Simple, **diatonic** chords – mainly triads in root position or first inversion, along with dominant 7ths in root position or inversion
- These simple chords are enlivened by frequent notes of melodic decoration, including occasional on-beat discords (**appoggiaturas** and **suspensions**) that 'resolve' by moving to a harmony note after the dissonance has sounded. In the following examples, the note in red is suspended from the previous chord while the small notes in blue are appoggiaturas:

- Tonic and dominant **pedals** underline the various changes of key in the central B section.
- Each of the three main sections ends with a prominent **perfect cadence** (in the key of D major in bars 77–78 and 309–310, and in B minor in bars 231–232).

Test yourself

1. Bach composed the Brandenburg concertos in the years leading up to 1721. In which musical period was this?

   i. **Baroque** ii. **Classical** iii. **Romantic** iv. **Modern**

2. Each Brandenburg concerto is written for a group of soloists accompanied by a small orchestra. What is the full name for this genre of music?
3. Name the three solo instruments in Brandenburg Concerto No. 5.
4. What is meant by the 'ripieno'?
5. Describe two musical features typical of a gigue.
6. Name one bass instrument and one chordal instrument that might play a basso continuo part.
7. Explain what is meant by realising a figured bass.
8. Identify the following in the last movement of Brandenburg concerto No. 5:

   a. **structure**

   b. **texture**

9. Name the key that is the relative minor of D major.
10. Complete the following sentence:

    The key of F♯ minor is the ________________ key of B minor.

11. What is the name for a passage of music in which imitative entries occur more closely than previously?
12. Name two types of ornament that occur in the last movement of Brandenburg Concerto No. 5.
13. What is meant by diatonic?
14. What essential word is missing from this definition?

    A sequence is the repetition of a melody or chord progression at a different pitch.

Answers: See page 69

Set work 2

Beethoven: Piano Sonata No. 8 in C minor Op. 13, 'Pathétique' (1st movement)

Context

By 1770, the Baroque style had given way to the elegance of the Classical period and the piano was replacing the harpsichord as the keyboard instrument of choice. Its full name (*pianoforte*) revealed its superiority over the harpsichord – individual notes can be played loudly or softly, allowing rapid contrasts in dynamics, sudden accents and effects such as *crescendo* and *diminuendo*. The most important composers of the Classical period were Haydn, Mozart, Beethoven and Schubert.

Ludwig van Beethoven was born in the German city of Bonn in 1770. At the age of 21 he moved to Vienna, capital of Austria, where he established a reputation as a **virtuoso** pianist, improvising and playing his own compositions as well as works by others, in public and private concerts. Beethoven won the support of the Viennese nobility which he acknowledged by dedicating his published works to the aristocrats who funded him. The set work is one of seven pieces dedicated to Prince Karl von Lichnowsky, a music lover in charge of the household of the Imperial Austrian Court and one of Beethoven's most generous sponsors.

In 1796, three years before the set work was published, Beethoven first reported the problems with his hearing that would eventually lead to his total deafness by about 1820. Despite this he could still hear music in his mind, and he composed some of his finest works when partially or even totally deaf. Many of these prefigure features of the new Romantic style that would start to emerge in his lifetime.

Beethoven's reputation spread quickly and by the age of 35 he was the most famous composer of instrumental music in Europe. His music has been frequently performed ever since, and today he is regarded as one of the greatest composers of all time.

Genre

The first movement of a piano sonata. During and after the Classical period the term sonata was used for works in three or four movements, each different in mood but related in key, written for either piano alone or for a solo instrument (such as a flute or violin) with piano.

Unlike piano concertos, which were performed in concert halls with orchestral accompaniment, sonatas were usually heard in the home. Simpler works were typically played by the daughters of aristocratic families in Vienna, who often had lessons from the leading musicians of the city, including Mozart and Beethoven. More difficult compositions (such as the set work) were intended for performance to small, invited audiences by celebrated pianists in the private musical soirées that were held in the glittering salons of the Viennese nobility.

Beethoven wrote 32 piano sonatas. No.8 is in three movements (fast-slow-fast) and was published in 1799 under the title *Grande Sonate Pathétique*. The French word *pathétique* means 'passionate' or 'emotional' and reflects a feature of the music that seems to anticipate the Romantic style of the 19th century.

The work was generally well received, although the violent energy, tragic passion and extreme contrasts in the music were dismissed as eccentric by some of the more conservative musicians of the day.

Resources

The pianos of Beethoven's day had wooden frames that could not support the high tension strings used on the iron-framed pianos of today. As a result, the tone was lighter and less sonorous than that of the modern grand piano (the latter is heard on the Anthology recording).

The first movement of the 'Pathétique' spans a range of five octaves (F to F, shown left), which is almost all of the 5½-octave compass available on pianos of the day.

Beethoven exploits this with:

- Long and rapid descents (bars 10 and 187–195)
- Wide leaps (bars 51–52 and 131–132)
- Use of different **registers** (e.g. both hands in the treble clef in bars 113–116, both in the bass clef in bars 167–171).

Beethoven also uses a wide dynamic range, from ***pp*** to ***ff***, with sudden contrasts, use of *crescendo* and *decrescendo* (*diminuendo*) and occasional forceful accents.

Beethoven's piano writing includes the need for the right hand to cross over the left (e.g. for the first four notes in bars 51–52 and in many similar places), wide separation of the hands (e.g. as the hands gradually move apart in **contrary motion** in bars 93–98) and thick, dense chords in the low register such as at the start of bar 133.

Period

Classical (Classical with a capital C refers to the music written in the period between about 1750 and 1825), but this sonata has features that look forward to the Romantic style of the 19th century, including:

- Emotional outbursts (justifying the name 'Pathétique')
- Extreme contrasts in dynamics and adventurous choice of keys
- Unusual structure (outlined below), in which the music of the slow introduction returns to twice interrupt the furious progress of the first movement.

Structure

The first movement (and sometimes one or more other movements) of almost all sonatas and other multi-movement works composed at this time was written in sonata form.

This has three main sections:

- **Exposition** (which introduces the first **subject** in the tonic key and the second subject in the dominant or other related key)
- **Development** (in which ideas from the exposition are transformed and taken through keys that are more distant from the tonic)
- **Recapitulation** (in which the music of the exposition returns, but altered to now stay mainly in the tonic key).

The first movement of the 'Pathétique' Sonata starts with a **slow introduction**. This was rare in piano sonatas, although it features in some Classical symphonies. Beethoven may have copied the idea from Clementi, whose piano sonata in G minor (Op. 34, No. 2) had just been published in 1795. It, too, starts with a slow introduction that features dotted rhythms and that unusually returns in the development.

The sub-sections of sonata form shown in the table on the following pages are:

- The **transition** (or bridge passage), which links the first and second subjects (it modulates to the related key in the exposition but has to be changed to remain in the tonic for the recapitulation)
- The **codetta** (or closing section), which ends the exposition by affirming the related key to which the music has modulated
- The **coda** (literally, 'tail'), which ends the movement by affirming its tonic key.

Often, the first subject in the tonic is forceful and the second subject in the related key is more lyrical. However, they can be very similar because it is the contrast in keys rather than melodies that is the most important feature of the exposition. The whole exposition is usually marked to be repeated.

Sonata form can be thought of as a journey in which someone leaves home (the tonic key), reaches a nearby destination (the related key) and then travels farther and farther away in the development, before safely returning for the recapitulation, where everything settles into the security of the home key.

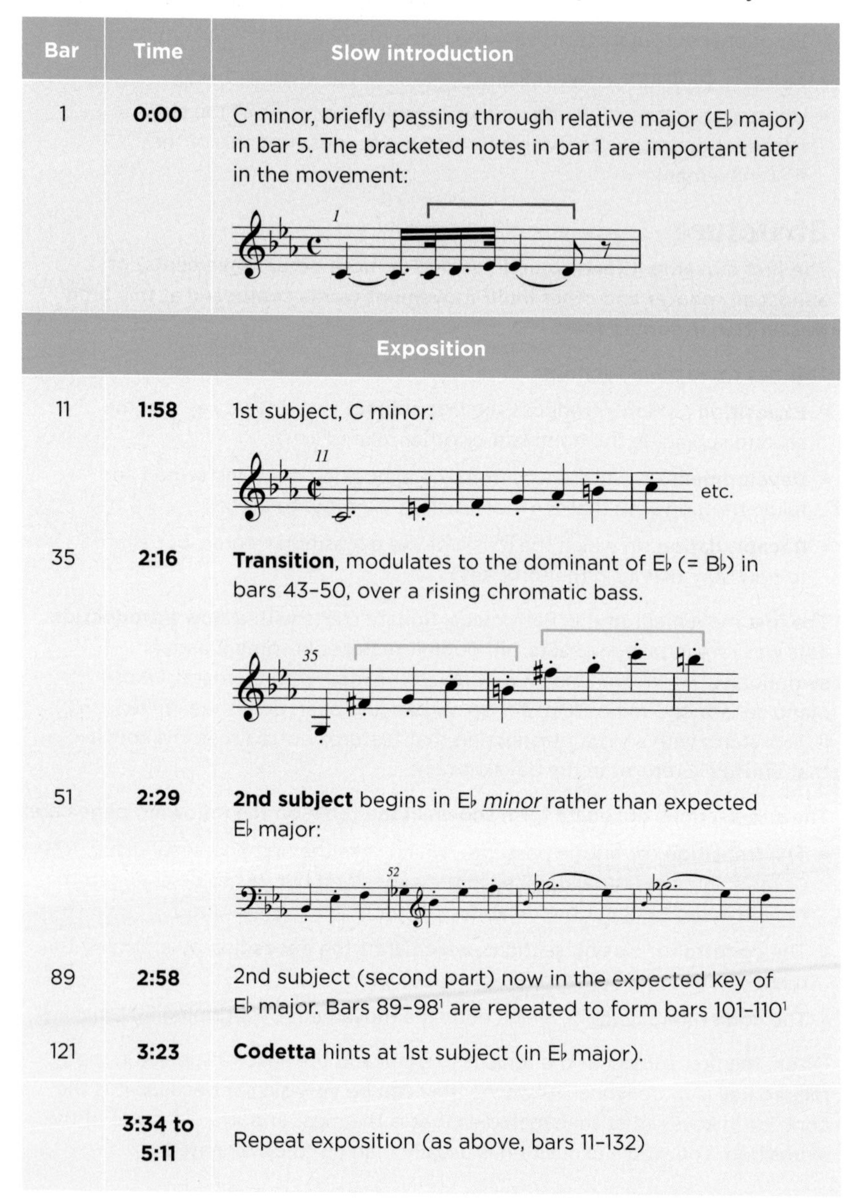

Bar	Time	Slow introduction
1	**0:00**	C minor, briefly passing through relative major (E♭ major) in bar 5. The bracketed notes in bar 1 are important later in the movement:
		Exposition
11	**1:58**	1st subject, C minor: etc.
35	**2:16**	**Transition**, modulates to the dominant of E♭ (= B♭) in bars 43–50, over a rising chromatic bass.
51	**2:29**	**2nd subject** begins in E♭ <u>minor</u> rather than expected E♭ major:
89	**2:58**	2nd subject (second part) now in the expected key of E♭ major. Bars 89–98[1] are repeated to form bars 101–110[1]
121	**3:23**	**Codetta** hints at 1st subject (in E♭ major).
	3:34 to 5:11	Repeat exposition (as above, bars 11–132)

Development		
133	**5:12**	Material from the opening of the slow introduction returns in G minor. An **enharmonic** change (E♭, bar 134 = D♯, bar 135) leads to an abrupt modulation to E minor.
137	**5:56**	Adaptations of transition theme welded to a fast version of the bracketed notes from the introduction, all in the remote key of E minor:  Octave figure from the bass of the 1st subject moves to the right hand in bar 149. Modulations through D major to G minor lead to...
167	**6:20**	28 bars of **dominant preparation**, with dominant pedal on G in bars 167–187, followed by a cascade of descending quavers that leads to...

Recapitulation		
195	**6:42**	Return of 1st subject in tonic key (C minor), modified from bar 207 to form a four-bar sequence that ends on a chord of C major in bar 219, leading to...
221	**7:02**	2nd subject, unexpectedly in F minor (IV of the tonic key) before moving to the conventional tonic key of C minor.
253	**7:28**	Bars 253–288 are a varied repeat of bars 89–124, now in the tonic key of C minor.
295	**8:06**	**Coda**: material from the slow introduction with its loud first-beat chords removed, followed by a final reference to 1st subject in tonic key (bar 299). Loud detached chords bring the movement to an end in a stormy perfect cadence.

Melody

Beethoven is famed for his skill in creating music from short motifs. In just the first eight bars of the slow introduction, the six-note motif bracketed below:

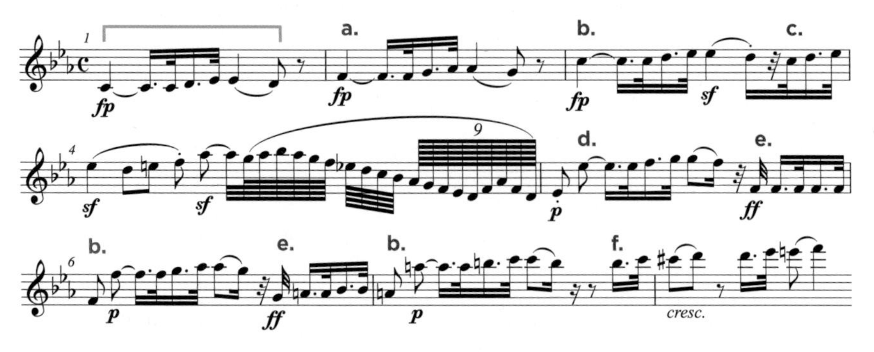

a. Is used in sequence in bar 2.

b. Has its last note reduced in length in bar 3 so that it can re-enter later in the same bar at (c). A similar process occurs in bars 6 and 7.

c. Is shortened to five notes by removing its first note.

d. Gains a syncopated start and has its last two notes halved in length.

e. Is reduced to just a reminder of its dotted rhythm.

f. Is decreased to just four notes, with its last two notes now rising, and this new four-note version now treated in rising sequence.

The slow introduction also includes scale passages, as in bar 4 above, and it ends with a rapid descending **chromatic** scale in bar 10.

The first subject is formed from an ascending scale of C minor, with its second degree (D) omitted and the third degree raised by a semitone to E♮. These two bars are repeated an octave higher and then balanced by four bars of longer notes (a 2+2+4-bar phrase structure). This balanced **periodic phrasing** is typical of the Classical style and here it creates an arch shape:

Beethoven's use of tiny melodic cells is seen again in the transition, starting at bar 35. Rising and falling semitones alternate as they climb and are then **augmented** (doubled in length) from bar 45 onward as the overall pitch descends:

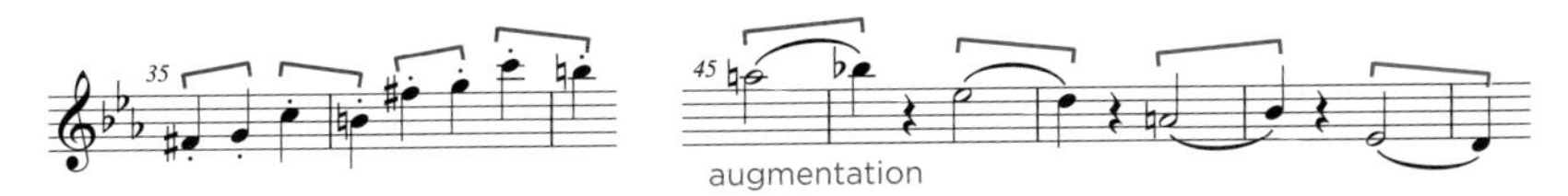

The second subject has a wide compass but again consists of a pair of balanced four-bar phrases, each starting on the second crotchet of a bar with four rising notes in the bass clef. The first ends with an imperfect cadence and the second with a perfect cadence. Complementary cadences like these are very common with periodic phrasing:

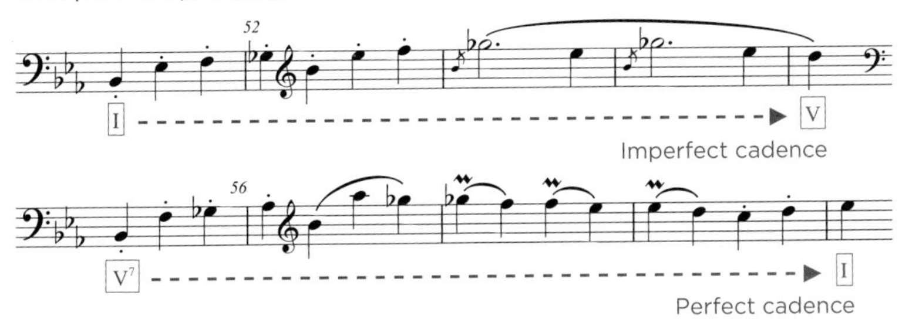

Notice how bars 56–8 are basically a decorated scale. The figuration in bars 93–98[1] (and in its repetition eight bars later) produces its exciting effect through the rising chromatic scale (again with a couple of small gaps) outlined by its top notes at the start of each minim beat. Beethoven also uses broken-chord patterns, such as those in bars 29–30 (repeated four bars later).

Ornaments used by Beethoven in this movement are:

- The **acciaccatura** (printed as a small note with a slash through the stem, as in bars 53–54 above, and played as quickly as possible)
- The **mordent** (marked 𝆘, as in bars 57–58 and played as a single rapid wiggle from the printed note to the note above and back)
- The **trill** (marked ***tr***, as in bars 182, 184 and 186, and played as a rapid and continuous wiggle between the printed note and the note above).

Metre and tempo

The introduction is in simple quadruple metre (the time signature C means the same as $\frac{4}{4}$). The tempo marking (*grave*) means very slow.

When the slow introduction returns in bar 133, the instruction 'Tempo I' tells the pianist to return to the opening tempo of the movement (i.e. *grave*).

The main part of the movement is in simple duple metre (the time signature ¢ means the same as $\frac{2}{2}$ and indicates two minim beats per bar). This is sometimes described as **alla breve** or 'cut-C' time.

The tempo of the alla breve sections is marked *Allegro molto e con brio*, which means very fast and with vigour.

Rhythm

- **Dotted rhythms** and **very short notes** feature in the introduction
- Occasional **syncopation** occurs among the **staccato crotchets** of the *Allegro* (e.g. bars 13, 19, 21 and the notes marked ***sf*** in bars 27 and 28)
- The constant quaver octaves in long sections of the left-hand part create the effect of an **ostinato**.
- Some passages consist of persistent quavers in both hands to drive the music forward (e.g. bars 89–112).

Tonality

The key is C minor with modulations to related keys (E♭, which is the relative major and G minor, the dominant) as well as to remote keys such as E minor, as shown in the table on pages 14 and 15. The 28 bars of dominant preparation for the recapitulation include a long dominant pedal on G in bars 167–187.

Harmony

Classical harmony is sometimes very simple - see the previous music example of the second subject in which the harmony moves from I to V in the first four bars, forming an imperfect cadence, and then from V^7 to I in the next four bars, creating a perfect cadence.

Other distinctive cadences include the interrupted cadence in bar 9 and the perfect cadence at the very end of the movement.

Beethoven also often uses chromatic chords, such as the **diminished 7th** on the first beat of bars 2, 3 and 4, and the augmented 6th (A♭ – C – F♯) in the second half of bars 30 and 34.

Texture

Homophonic - densely chordal at the start of the introduction followed by melody-and-accompaniment in the *Allegro*, where the texture is often thinner (e.g. bars 93–98 have a two-part texture, while bars 187^2–194 are monophonic).

Note the use of **broken octaves ('murky bass')** in the left hand of the first subject and **broken chords** in the passage beginning at bar 93 (second half of second subject). The start of the second subject is in the bass clef, requiring the pianist to cross hands.

Dynamics

Beethoven's markings are much more extensive than those of earlier composers and include rapid contrasts (e.g. ***p*-*ff*-*p*-*ff*-*p*** in bars 5–7, with ***pp*** in bar 88), gradual changes (crescendo and decrescendo (= diminuendo)), and frequent sudden accents on notes marked ***sfz*** (*sforzando*, meaning 'forced').

Test yourself

1. Put the following musical periods in order from earliest to latest:

   i. **Romantic** ii. **Baroque** iii. **Classical**

2. In which European capital city did Beethoven spend most of his working life?

3. Name two composers from the Classical period, other than Beethoven.

4. It was unusual to start a piano sonata with a slow introduction. What else is unusual about the slow introduction in the 'Pathétique' sonata?

5. Give the name of each of the following sections in sonata form:

   a. The passage that links the first and second subjects

   b. The section at the end of the exposition

   c. The main section that follows the development

6. a. Explain what is meant by dominant preparation.

   b. Where can an extended passage of dominant preparation be heard in the first movement of the 'Pathétique' sonata?

7. How should notes marked ***sf*** be played?

8. Name a type of chromatic chord that features in the first movement of the 'Pathétique' sonata.

9. a. In a sonata-form movement in C minor, the second subject would normally first appear in the key of E♭ major. In what key does the second subject start in the exposition of the 'Pathétique' sonata?

   b. In what key does the second subject start in the recapitulation of this same movement?

10. How should notes printed like this 𝆔 be played?

Answers: See page 69

AREA OF STUDY 2:
Vocal music

Vocal music includes any works that feature singing, from short songs to large-scale pieces for large choirs, with or without accompaniment.

For the purpose of the GCSE exam, the focus in this area of study is on songs for one or more solo voices with instrumental accompaniment. The first set work dates from 1692 while the second is a rock song from 1974, written nearly 300 years later.

Set work 1

Purcell: 'Music for a While'

Period and genre

Mid-Baroque. Solo song (with continuo accompaniment).

Context

Henry Purcell worked in London towards the end of the 17th century and is widely regarded as one of the greatest composers in the history of English music. Although he died at the age of only 36, he composed music for the church, the stage and for important royal occasions, and he wrote many shorter pieces, including songs and instrumental works.

'Music for a While' is **incidental music** – music intended to be performed as part of a play. It is about the power of music and is one of several songs Purcell wrote (probably in 1692) for *Oedipus*, a play by the leading poet of the late 17th century, John Dryden, and the dramatist Nathaniel Lee. It is loosely based on a classical Greek tragedy, *Oedipus Rex* (Oedipus the King), written in 430 BC.

In Dryden and Lee's play, 'Music for a While' is sung to raise the ghost of King Laius from the dead, in the hope of discovering the identity of his murderer (who turns out to be his son, Oedipus). Alecto was a minor deity from ancient Greece who avenged crimes. She was said to have snakes for hair and to torment the guilty with a studded whip. In Dryden's poem, music soothes her fury until she drops the whip and the snakes fall from her head.

Resources

- Solo voice and continuo (harpsichord and bass viol on the Anthology recording).
- Purcell wrote just a melody and an (unfigured) bass part for the song. He did not specify the type of voice, but in the play it was probably originally sung by a male singer with a high voice (either a tenor or countertenor)
- On the Anthology recording the music is transposed from its original key of C minor up to A minor, and is performed by a soprano. The bass part is played on a bass viol (a six-stringed predecessor of the cello) and is doubled by the harpsichordist's left hand. The right-hand of the harpsichord part is an elaborate realisation of the harmony implied by Purcell's bass.

Structure

Purcell constructed the song over a ground bass - a constantly repeating bass pattern above which a melody unfolds. It was a popular device in 17th-century music, especially in pieces by Purcell who was a master of the technique.

The ground in 'Music for a While' is three bars in length and is based on a four-note sequence formed from rising 5ths alternating with falling 6ths. It climbs from the tonic to the dominant of A minor (from A to E, printed in red below):

The ground is heard 12 times in succession, but Purcell avoids monotony by modulating to related keys in the middle (B) section of the song, changing the length of the ground in the process, as shown below:

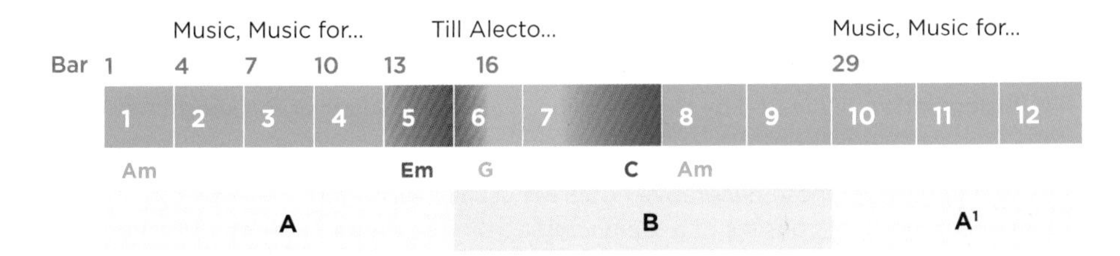

The opening music, set to the opening words, returns in bar 29 to create an overall ternary form (ABA¹) for the song:

- The first (A) section is in the key of A minor, ending with a modulation to the dominant key (E minor)
- The middle (B) section is characterised by modulations through related keys, and by shortened and lengthened versions of the ground bass

- The final section returns to A minor and is labelled A¹ above to show that the singer on the Anthology recording ornaments the original melody for this repeat and that Purcell extended the ending in order to finish on the tonic chord.

Tonality

The song is in A minor, with modulations to related keys in the middle section, as described above.

The upper notes at the start of the ground bass (E - F - F♯ - G - G♯ - A) form a chromatic scale that sometimes leaves the tonality ambiguous, but modulations are always confirmed by perfect cadences.

Melody

The vocal melody:

- Combines stepwise movement with occasional leaps
- Contains frequent **passing notes** between chord notes
- Has a **range** of just over an octave, from E above middle C to the F a minor 9th higher (the top G in bar 36 is not by Purcell)
- Incorporates rests for expressive effect
- Includes both rising sequences (e.g. on 'Wond'ring' in bars 10–12) and falling sequences (e.g. on 'eas'd' in bars 13–15).

The many ornaments in the soprano and right-hand harpsichord parts are not by Purcell but have been added by the performers, following the style commonly used in Baroque slow movements. They include:

- **Upper mordents** (indicated by 𝆖, e.g. in bar 11)
- **Lower mordents** (indicated by 𝆗, e.g. in bar 11)
- **Appoggiaturas** (indicated by a note printed in small type in e.g. bar 5)
- **Slides** and **grace notes** (e.g. the notes in small type in bar 6)
- **Trills** (indicated by ***tr*** above the vocal stave in bar 13)
- **Arpeggiation** (indicated by the wavy line in e.g. the last bar of the song).

Apart from the appoggiatura (which usually takes at least half the value of the note that follows) these decorative notes are usually very short. For example, the upper mordent consists of a rapid wiggle from the printed note to the note above and back, while the trill consists of a rapid repeated alternation of the printed note with the note a step above. The arpeggio sign indicates that the notes of the chord are played in rapid succession, from low to high, instead of sounding together.

As in many of his ground bass songs, Purcell avoids predictability by sometimes continuing the vocal phrase beyond the end of the ground so that the two parts do not always end their phrases together:

(The notes in red above are suspensions, explained below.)

Word setting and word painting

- The word setting is mainly **syllabic**, but Purcell uses a **melisma** for the words 'wond'ring' (= wondering) and 'eternal'
- Purcell frequently repeats words in the text, such as 'Music' at the start, 'all' in bars 7–9 and 'drop' (sung nine times in succession in bars 23–25).

The many examples of word-painting in this song include:

- The rising chromaticism and eerily angular outline of the ground bass, suggesting the spirit of Laius rising from his bones
- Six repetitions of 'all', separated by rests, to suggest a multitude (bars 7–9, with even more repetitions in the final bars of the song)
- Melismas to illustrate the contemplative nature of 'wond'ring' (bars 10–11)
- A suspension to create a harsh discord on 'pains' in bar 12 (E in the voice clashes with the accompanying chord of D minor), followed by...
- A chain of suspensions in bars 13–14, where the resolution of each dissonance onto a warm consonance repeatedly occurs on the word 'eased'. These dissonant notes are shown in red in the example above
- The words 'free the dead' in bars 16–17 are set to one of the few ascending phrases in the song, and are in the more cheerful key of G major
- The word 'eternal' in bars 19–21 is set to long melismas that keep winding around the same few notes to portray the everlasting nature of death
- Purcell repeats the word 'drop' on quaver off-beats nine times in bars 23–25, to suggest the snakes dropping away from Alecto's head.

Rhythm and dynamics

The music is in simple quadruple metre ($\frac{4}{4}$ time).

The rhythm of the ground bass is entirely in quavers, creating a steady tread known as a **walking bass** that doesn't cease until the final bar of the entire song.

The vocal part follows the rhythm of the words and is written mainly in quavers and semiquavers, with **syncopation** for the off-beat notes on 'drop' in bars 23–25. Tied notes and dotted rhythms appear in the right-hand harpsichord part. In common with much music written before 1700 there are no dynamic or expression markings and no tempo is specified – decisions on these matters were left to the performers. The nature of the **lyrics**, along with the continuous quaver pulse of the ground, suggest that the music is counted in quavers, eight to the bar, which will result in a slow tempo.

Texture

- Homophonic texture (melody and accompaniment)
- The elaborate harpsichord realisation sometimes creates counterpoint with the vocal part, including some short imitative points, such as in bars 9 and 11 (in which the accompanist's right-hand part anticipates the descending scales in the vocal part, so that the singer appears to be imitating the accompaniment).

Harmony

The chord progression dictated by the ground bass mainly consists of alternate root-position and first-inversion triads:

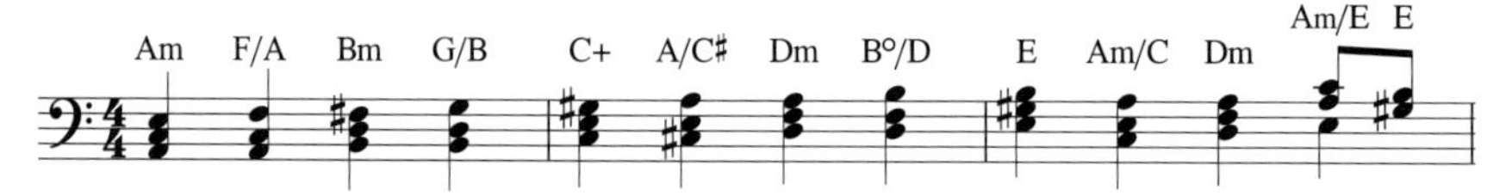

The + symbol indicates an augmented triad (the interval from C to G♯ is an augmented 5th) and ° indicates a diminished triad.

Similar chords are used even when Purcell transposes and extends the pattern in the middle of the song. Variety comes from the changing layouts and decorations provided by the harpsichordist, and in the different passing notes and suspensions introduced into the vocal part.

The realisation contains examples of one of the fingerprints of 16th- and 17th-century English music. Called a **false relation**, it consists of two different forms of the same pitch occurring in different parts together or in close proximity. In the example below, the notes F♯ in the left hand and F(♮) in the right hand of bar 1, form a false relation, as do the notes G♯ in the left hand and G(♮) in the right hand of bar 2:

Another feature of 17th-century English harmony occurs on the third beat of bar 23, where the chord of A major instead of A minor on 'snakes' forms a **tierce de Picardie** – a major tonic chord ending a cadence in a minor key.

Test yourself

1. What type of instrument is a bass viol?

   i. **Woodwind** ii. **Brass** iii. **String** iv. **Percussion** v. **Keyboard**

2. In which century did Purcell live?

3. The structure of 'Music for a While' can be represented by the letters ABA^1. What name is given to this form?

4. Name ***two*** ways, other than lyrics, in which the B section of this song differs from the A sections.

5. What are the ***two*** main types of word setting in vocal music?

6. Name the device shown by the bracketed notes.

7. Name ***two*** types of ornament used in 'Music for a While'.

8. Give ***three*** examples of word painting from 'Music for a While'.

9. What name is given to a note that is held over from a previous chord to form a dissonance and that then resolves by moving to a note of the new chord?

10. What is incidental music?

11. Circle ***two*** notes in the example below that form a false relation.

Answers: See page 69

Set work 2

'Killer Queen' (from the Queen album *Sheer Heart Attack*)

Context

The rock group Queen was formed in London in 1970–71 by four college students, all of whom would go on to write hit songs for the band:

Freddie Mercury	(lead singer and pianist)
Brian May	(lead guitar and backing vocals)
Roger Taylor	(drums and backing vocals)
John Deacon	(bass guitar)

'Killer Queen', a song about a high-class prostitute who enjoys eating caviar and drinking Moët and Chandon champagne, was written by Freddie Mercury and is a track from Queen's third studio album (and first major success), *Sheer Heart Attack*, released in 1974.

Freddie Mercury (1946–1991) was the stage name of Farrokh Bulsara, born to Persian parents on the island of Zanzibar, East Africa. From the age of eight he was sent to an English boarding school in India, where he learnt the piano and played in the school's rock and roll band. When Mercury was 17, he moved with his family to Feltham in west London. He studied at Ealing College of Art, but already his thoughts were turning towards a career in music.

Although Queen were part of the succession of British male groups that followed in the footsteps of the Beatles and the Rolling Stones, by the early 1970s rock had diversified into various sub-genres, including progressive rock (sometimes called art rock) which was a major influence on Queen's earliest work. However, the band is now known for the range of its musical styles, from piano-based pop and songs that evoke 1950s' rockabilly and 1920s' vaudeville, to power ballads and hard rock numbers, all presented in well-crafted arrangements with expert production techniques, and often featuring vocals in four-part **close harmony** and **overdubbed** guitar parts. Their best-known track is the six-minute long *Bohemian Rhapsody* (1975), but they are also remembered for sing-along anthems such as *We Will Rock You* and *We Are the Champions* (both 1977).

Date and genre

'Killer Queen' was written in 1974 and is a rock song.

Queen adopted a style of performance popular at the time that is known as glam rock. It involved male performers with big hairstyles, dressed in flamboyant clothes with glitter and wearing boots with platform soles. Presentation included a large drum kit mounted high on a platform called a drum riser, state-of-the-art stage effects such as smoke, dry ice, fireworks and elaborate lighting. Despite all this, Queen were particularly interested in the use of studio effects, even though some of these were difficult or impossible to recreate in their live performances. Although synthesisers were available at the time, Queen did not use them until the 1980s.

Resources

Lead vocal, piano and most of the backing vocals (including the overdubbed three- and four-part harmony in the chorus) are all performed by Freddie Mercury. Mercury overdubbed the piano part with the same music played on a 'honky-tonk' or 'jangle' piano, in which tacks in the hammers create a tinny, retro effect.

Freddie Mercury was famed for the quality and range of his voice, with its ability to glide effortlessly between high tenor and falsetto (listen for falsetto in bars 11–13). In this song he covers a range of two octaves and a 3rd:

Brian May played guitar (again with much overdubbing to produce the parts marked Gtr 2, 3 and 4 in the score). Roger Taylor played drums and John Deacon played bass guitar. Much of the bass guitar part doubles the left hand of the piano part and so is not shown separately in the Anthology score, but listen for features such as the prominent descending bass-guitar scale in bar 38.

Listen for two additional percussion instruments: a triangle (heard on the first beat of bar 29) and windchimes (struck on the word 'you' in bar 68).

Like most pop and jazz, 'Killer Queen' was not originally written in music notation. The score in the Anthology was made by writing down what is played on the recording – a type of score known as a **transcription**. It includes several special signs and abbreviations:

~~	e.g. bar 7	**Vibrato** - continual small fluctuations of pitch to warm the sound of a note
8va----	e.g. bar 19	**An ottava sign** - a direction that the notes sound an octave higher than written
♩ (tremolo strokes)	e.g. bar 26 and bar 28	**Tremolo** - a rapid repetition of a note, indicating a cymbal roll in bar 26 and a snare drum roll in bar 28
^	e.g. bar 30	**Pitch bend** - a small slide in pitch away from a note and back again
—	e.g. bar 34	**Slide** - a smooth glide in pitch from one note to the next
P.M.	bar 69	**Palm Mute** - damping the strings with the side of the hand while plucking to produce a very dark, dry sound

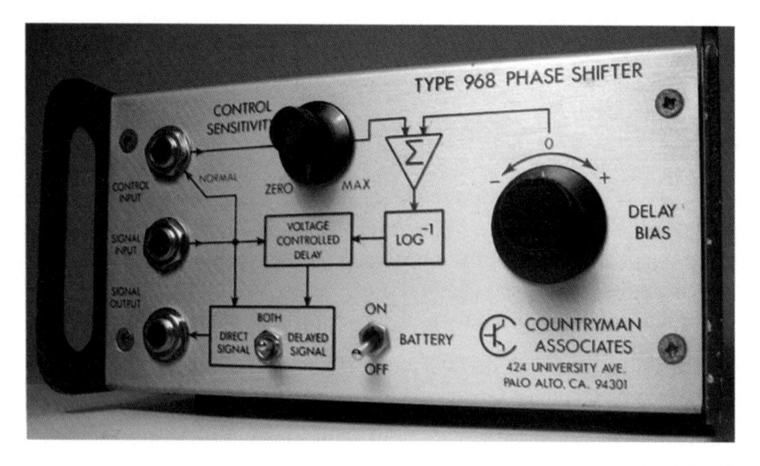

A Countryman Phase Shifter

Queen enthusiastically embraced the latest studio technology in their recordings. In 'Killer Queen' sound engineer Roy Thomas Baker reported that the distinctive sound on the words 'laser beam' in bar 17 was produced by a Countryman **Phase Shifter**, a device that had appeared on the market only a few months before the recording.

In addition to the extensive use of **overdubbing** to produce the multiple guitar tracks (all played by Brian May) and four-part vocals in the chorus (all sung by Freddie Mercury) there is **reverb** on the lead vocal, but not on the backing vocals (so the latter sounds as tight as possible, aided by treble boost and compression) and carefully controlled **distortion** on the solo guitar part. Note the use of a **wah-wah** effect in the guitar parts of bar 62. Sounds are carefully panned in the stereo mix (listen for 'anytime' in the backing vocals being **panned** hard right in bar 19 and similar places, and for the stereo separation of the overlapping guitar parts in bars 55–6 and at the end of the song).

Structure

'Killer Queen' is in verse-and-chorus form, as shown in the table, below. The small superscript numbers indicate beats (so 2^4 means bar 2, beat 4).

The section labelled 'instrumental' in bars 23–26 of the Anthology is merely a four-bar link from the end of the first chorus to the start of the second verse The guitar solo in bars 44–61^3 replaces the voice in the second part of Chorus 2 and the first part of Verse 3 and would more usually be described as an instrumental:

Bar 2^3	0:02	Verse 1	
Bar 14^4	0:27	Chorus 1	
Bar 23	0:44	Instrumental	
Bar 26^4	0:51	Verse 2	
Bar 38^4	1:15	Chorus 2	**Guitar solo** (Bars 44 to 61) (1:25 to 2:00)
Bar 51	1:40	Verse 3	
Bar 69^2	2:16	Chorus 3	
Bar 79	2:35	Outro	

The six finger-clicks that set the tempo and overlap with the start of the vocal are just a lead-in – they are too insubstantial to be called an introduction.

Melody

- The melody initially moves by step and small intervals, but the leaps get progressively wider (e.g. a rising 6th in bars 6–7 and 10–11, and a rising octave in bars 20–21).

- The verses start with a two-bar vocal phrase that is repeated with its ending changed to finish on a climactic top G rather than on C:

- To avoid predictability, the next phrase is extended to five bars by the insertion of a $\frac{6}{8}$ bar (bar 10).
- Bar 12 is repeated in a modified rising **sequence** to form Bar 13. The same **falling-5th motif** is used in the chorus, where it forms a modified falling sequence in bars 20–21:

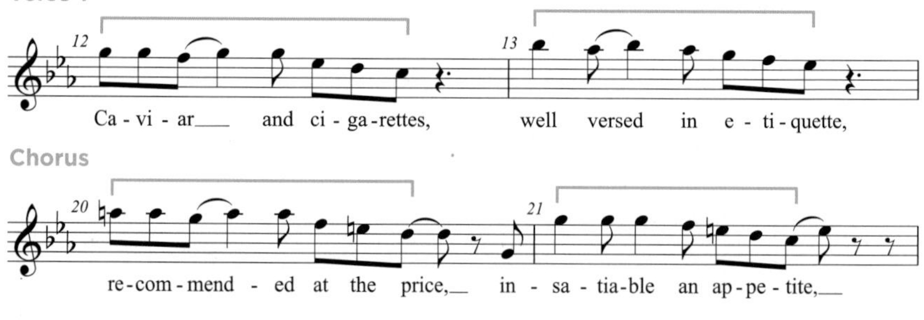

- Notice the use of **portamento** on the word 'queen' in bar 15.
- Unusual phrase lengths occur again in the chorus, where its eight bars are structured as five bars followed by three bars.
- The chorus is followed by a four-bar instrumental bridge (or link).
- Every verse and chorus begins with an **anacrusis** (known as a pickup in pop and jazz), as shown in the first example on this page.

The rest of the song follows a similar pattern, with small changes in the melody to accommodate different words and some extra detail to provide variety. Changes are a little more extensive in the guitar solo, which replaces the voice in the second part of chorus 2 and the first part of verse 3. The outro is based on the link that follows the choruses.

- The word setting is almost entirely syllabic, with occasional spoken text (shown by x-headed notes, e.g. in bar 38).
- The backing vocals sometimes include **vocables** (nonsense syllables, such as 'ooh' in bars 8–11 and 'ba, ba, ba, ba' in bar 18).

- There is little word painting, other than the upward slide to emphasise the sarcastic use of 'queen' in the chorus, the phaser effect to make 'laser beam' sound unworldly two bars later and the climactic top notes and busy drum part for 'absolutely drive you wild' in bars 66–67.

Rhythm

- Most of the song is in compound quadruple metre - four dotted-crotchet beats (= 12 quavers) per bar - giving the rhythm a **swing** feel.
- The tempo is moderately fast, at 112 dotted-crotchet beats per minute.
- There is frequent use of **syncopation** (e.g. the tied notes in bars 3, 7, 8 etc).
- Each verse and chorus begins with an **anacrusis**.

Tonality

The song is in E♭ major but the tonality is sometimes ambiguous. Verses start in C minor and choruses are in B♭ major, but both quickly modulate.

However, the song does end with a perfect cadence in E♭ major and it fades out on the tonic chord of that key.

Harmony

- Mostly root position triads with occasional inversions and 7th chords. Chords are mainly diatonic, with occasional chromatic chords (e.g. A♭m in bar 9).
- Some use of expressive dissonance (e.g. G above a chord of B♭^{7} in the lead vocal of bar 11, resolving to the chord note of F).
- Short **tonic pedal** in C minor at the start of each verse and a **dominant pedal** (F in the key of B♭) in the instrumental links following the first two choruses.
- Freddie Mercury's multi-tracked backing vocals in bars 15–17 and elsewhere produce a succession of **parallel harmonies** in three and four parts.
- **Descending chromatic scale** from tonic to dominant of E♭ major in lead guitar, bass guitar and piano left hand in bars 7–9.
- **Circle of 5ths** progression in bars 20–21 (A - Dm - G^7 - C).
- Guitar parts in bar 55 produce **bell chords** (in which notes are sustained in downward succession instead of being played together).

Texture

- **Homophonic**, gradually increasing in density from a very light-textured start.
- **Chordal** texture for the vocals at the start and end of the chorus.
- Guitar parts in parallel 3rds in the link following the first chorus (bars 23–26).
- Brief contrapuntal fragments in the accompaniment (e.g. in bar 62, where guitar 4 imitates the lead vocal, and during the fade-out).

Test yourself

1. Name a hit by Queen, other than 'Killer Queen'.
2. Name the instrument that plays throughout most of 'Killer Queen' but that does not have a separate part shown in the Anthology score.
3. What is an anacrusis?
4. Complete this sentence: In 12/8 time there are ___________ dotted-crotchet beats per bar.
5. How are the x-headed notes ( ) in the score of 'Killer Queen' performed?
6. What is the technical name for a vocal slide in pitch, such as that heard on the word 'queen' in this song?
7. The sign ~~~~ in the score shows where the lead guitarist uses vibrato. What is vibrato?
8. Name the vocal technique used by Freddie Mercury to sing the highest notes in 'Killer Queen'.
9. What name can be used to describe the chord progression A – Dm – G^7 – C?
10. What are vocables?
11. Why are the following described as parallel chords?

Answers: See page 70

AREA OF STUDY 3:
Music for stage and screen

Music and drama have been partners since ancient times and are still closely linked today. We know that music was heard in the mystery plays of medieval Europe and that song played an important part in the works of Shakespeare. Almost a century later, 'Music for a While' was one of many songs written by Purcell for inclusion in the plays of his day.

When Shakespeare was writing in the years around 1600, **opera** was invented in Italy – drama sung and acted on stage by professional singers accompanied by an orchestra. A lighter type of opera known as **operetta** ('little opera') developed in the late-19th century, in which spoken dialogue alternated with musical items, and this paved the way for the 20th-century **musical** – a play or film with music in a broadly popular style that generally includes some memorable hit songs.

Set work 1

Stephen Schwartz: 'Defying Gravity' (from the musical *Wicked*)

Context, date and genre

One of the best-loved musical films of the 20th century was *The Wizard of Oz* (1939), based on the *The Wonderful Wizard of Oz*, an American children's novel of 1900 by L. Frank Baum.

In 1995, American author Gregory Maguire produced a fantasy novel entitled *Wicked: The Life and Times of the Wicked Witch of the West.* It retells the original story from the point of view of the witches, Elphaba (The Wicked Witch of the West) and Glinda, who Maguire casts as The Good Witch of the North. It creates a back-story for many of the other characters in *Oz* and explores the nature of good and evil.

Maguire's novel was turned into the **book** (the spoken dialogue of a musical) by the American screenwriter Winnie Holzman to form the basis of *Wicked,* a musical first staged in the USA, in 2003. The **lyrics** (the words of the songs) and the music are by Stephen Schwartz (born 1948) whose other credits include the 1971 musical *Godspell* and the lyrics for Disney's animated musical film *Pocahontas* (1995).

'Defying Gravity' is the Act One **finale** (the last number in the first half of the show) in which Elphaba, who has discovered that the Wizard of Oz is a charlatan, vows to oppose his evil plans. The song describes how she wants to live life without limits, going against the rules that others have set for her. The song includes short duet sections with Glinda, **underscore** (music played under dialogue), and a short part for the chorus at the end. This composite format is sometimes called a **scena** ('scene'). The staging is highly dramatic, culminating in Elphaba flying into the air on her broomstick, accompanied by moving lights, smoke and wind effects as the citizens of Oz rush in, trying in vain to 'bring her down'.

Structure

The core of *Defying Gravity* is a song in verse-and-chorus form. In the table below, recitative is a type of vocal music that mimics the rhythms of speech.

Bar	Time	Section
1	0:04	**Intro** (*recitative for Glinda and Elphaba*): 'I hope you're happy...'
34²	1:17	**Verse 1** (*Elphaba*): 'Something has changed within me, ...'
50²	1:51	**Chorus** (*Elphaba*): 'It's time to try defying gravity...' *(Glinda sings the link at bar 60)*
63²	2:10	**Verse 2** (*Elphaba*): 'I'm through accepting limits...'
79²	2:35	**Chorus** (*Elphaba*): 'I'd sooner try defying gravity...' *(Glinda sings the link at bar 60)*
88	2:48	**Bridge** (*Elphaba*): 'Unlimited, together...' *(+ Glinda from bar 100)*
102³	3:27	**Chorus** (*Elphaba and Glinda*): 'Just you and I defying gravity...' *(orchestral build at end)*

115[2]	3:53	**Varied reprise of intro** (*Glinda, then both*): 'I hope you're happy...'
135[2]	4:32	**Verse 3** (*Elphaba*): 'So if you care to find me' *(some parts 8ve higher than before)*
151[2]	4:58	**Chorus** (*Elphaba*): 'Tell them how I am defying gravity...'
161[4]	5:15	**Coda** (*Elphaba, then all*): 'And nobody in all of Oz...'

In the stage show, the finale is in D♭ major, a semitone lower than the version in the Anthology, and there are additional passages of underscore.

Resources

The accompaniment is scored by specialist orchestrator Bill Brohn for a relatively large pit band of 23 musicians. The four woodwind ('reed') players have to double on a variety of instruments (including piccolo, bass clarinet and cor anglais).

There are six brass, a harp, two electric guitars, three keyboard synths, used partly to bolster the four string parts (a full body of strings is used for recordings) and a wide range of percussion, including drum kit, timpani, glockenspiel (a tuned percussion instrument with metal bars struck by beaters) and tubular bells.

The excerpt in the Anthology is in the form of a short score, which shows the main band parts on just two staves. Points to note in the orchestration include:

- Electric guitar with **overdrive** (a type of distortion) in bars 11, 40 and 45
- Chordal writing for low brass contrasting with solo synth melody (bars 20–23)
- String **tremolo** (marked ≡) to create excitement (bars 34–36 and 162–165)
- Drum **fill** (bar 54) – a brief improvisation to fill the gap between vocal phrases
- Descending scales for bass clarinet (bars 89 and 91)
- Cymbal roll to announce the change of key (bar 122)
- **Tutti** (full band) for the climax at bar 135
- Synth and glockenspiel play a high-pitched **ostinato** as Elphaba sings of flying high (bars 152–160).

The two principal singers, Elphaba and Glinda, require the vocal ranges shown below for this number. In the other parts of the show, Glinda has higher notes than the F♯ shown below. The character requires a **soprano** vocal range. Elphaba is a **mezzo-soprano**, a voice lower in range than a soprano but not as low as an alto.

Glinda Elphaba

There is a small part for the chorus (labelled 'ensemble') in the final bars.

Commentary

The direction *colla voce* ('with the voice') in bar 1 indicates that the band must follow the rhythm of the singers, which is fairly free.

In the introduction (bars 1–31) Glinda confronts Elphaba in **recitative** initially punctuated by chromatic **stabs** (loud detached chords). Elphaba answers her taunts by sarcastically mimicking them a semitone lower (bar 9). Hints of the change that is about to occur in Elphaba are heard in the underscore of bars 20–24, where the syncopated introductory chords to her song are first heard, but the juxtaposition of two totally unrelated keys (B major followed by F major) creates an unsettling effect. Glinda's reassurance that Elphaba can still be with the wizard is accompanied by comforting sustained harmonies in F major.

Elphaba's realisation that 'Something has changed within me' is underpinned by another sudden change of key in bar 32, this time to D major, the main key of 'Defying Gravity'. The song itself begins after a two-bar introduction.

Elphaba asserts her desire to break free from expectations in a 16-bar verse characterised by a number of determined, wide leaps initially accompanied by a nervous **tremolo** from violins (bars 34–39). The tempo tightens to ***Allegro*** in bar 49 as she moves towards the chorus, which features more angular leaps in the vocal line, many of which are **triadic**. High above the vocal line, a repeating accompaniment pattern of three ascending quavers (printed in small type in the Anthology) cuts across the beat from bar 51 onwards.

The introductory chords from bars 32–3 return in bar 59 and are repeated as an accompaniment to Glinda's accusation in crotchet triplets that Elphaba is having delusions of grandeur, but Elphaba defiantly continues into her second verse, at a faster tempo and with firmly syncopated accompaniment.

After the second chorus, the tempo relaxes (***Moderato*** in bar 88) and the key changes to G major. The melody in bars 93–94 quotes the first seven pitches of the song 'Over the Rainbow' from the 1939 musical film, 'The Wizard of Oz':

This 'unlimited' melody is a **leitmotif** that reflects Elphaba's growing confidence and that permeates the musical.

The *colla voce* direction in bar 99 marks a short passage of recitative in which Elphaba invites Glinda to join her and they begin the chorus together, starting at the end of bar 102, with just a little two-part singing before Elphaba finishes the chorus alone.

The introductory music from bar 32 returns in bars 111–114, this time leading to a recitative based on the chromatic chords of the opening bars of the scene. In a subtle change, Schwartz removes the word 'now' from the sarcastic 'I hope you're happy now", turning it into an affirmative 'I hope you're happy' as the friends wish each other well. The tempo returns to *Allegro* and the introductory syncopated motif to the verses is heard again in bars 129 and 132. The return of D major in bar 132 sees an exciting orchestral **build** (a *crescendo* on repeated quavers) during which the castle guards break in, only to see Elphaba soar above them on her broom as she launches into her triumphant final verse (starting at bar 135). Parts of this verse are sung an octave higher than previously.

The **coda** ('And nobody in all of Oz') begins quietly and at a slower pace (***Andante*** in Bar 162) but quickly crescendos into the final bars. Elphaba rises to her top note (F♯ on 'me' in bar 167) and from bar 169 to the end the people of Oz rush in and join with the guards in singing 'Look at her! She's wicked! Get her!'.

Texture

After some brief monophonic passages at the start, the texture is mainly melody and accompaniment. Schwartz included the simplest type of duet writing in which the two characters mainly sing either alternately or together in unison (e.g. bars 101–109).

There are just a couple of passages of very easy two-part vocal writing (e.g. parallel 3rds in bars 125–128), plus a brief contrapuntal section in the final bars. **Ostinato** figures occur in bars 80–87, 88–97, 103–109 and 152–159.

Tonality

The main parts of the song (verses and choruses) are in D major, with a section in G major in bars 88–100.

Chromatic writing at the start and in bars 115–131 creates areas of ambiguous tonality.

Harmony

The harmony includes root position triads and sus chords, in which the 3rd of the chord is replaced by either a 2nd above the root (sus^2) or a 4th (sus^4). For example, the chord in bar 60 is Gsus^2 (G – A – D), whereas a chord of G would be G – B – D).

There is an inner **pedal** on A in bars 162–167 followed by an inverted pedal on D, starting in bar 168.

Rhythm and melody

Recitative sections are in free time in which the speed is dictated by the singers. Elsewhere, there are many changes of tempo in the song, some associated with a 'rall.' (*rallentando*, meaning slowing down).

There is a minim beat ($\frac{2}{2}$ or $\frac{3}{2}$ time) until the $\frac{4}{4}$ in bar 88. $\frac{2}{2}$ returns in bar 115. Many vocal phrases start on a weak beat and the word setting is syllabic.

Syncopation plays an important role in the **rhythm** of 'Defying Gravity', particularly in the anticipation of strong beats by a quaver (a technique known as a **push** in pop music and jazz), as in bars 50–51:

Syncopation:

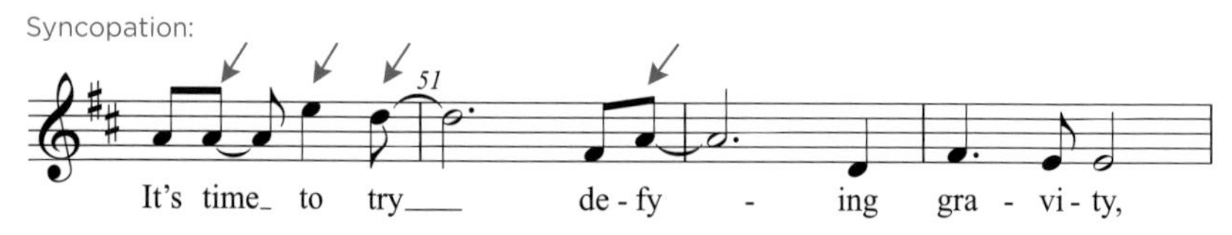

Notice the **triadic** style of Elphaba's vocal line in this example – most of the notes come from a triad of D major (D – F♯ – A). The long notes and wide leaps help to illustrate Elphaba's new-found confidence as the song unfolds. Intervals of a 4th and 5th feature prominently in the vocal line as Elphaba becomes increasingly sure of herself and even wider leaps appear as she becomes more determined, especially in bars 39–40 (a leap of an 11th) and bar 140 (a leap of a 12th).

The melody for 'try defying gravity' shown above is known as the **title hook** – in pop music, a hook is a melodic fragment designed to catch the ear of the listener, and is called the title hook when it includes the words of the song's title.

Test yourself

1. What is the term for music played under dialogue in musicals and films?
2. Give the meaning of the following directions:
   a. *colla voce*
   b. *rall.*
3. Describe the accompaniment in the first three bars of 'Defying Gravity'.
4. The vocal style at the start of 'Defying Gravity' is described as like recitative. What do you understand is meant by the term recitative?
5. How does the vocal melody in bar 7 relate to bar 6? ____ ?
6. How are the x-headed notes (𝅘𝅥 with x head) in the score of 'Defying Gravity' performed?
7. What type of effect is guitar overdrive?
8. What is an ostinato?
9. What is the approximate range of the two solo vocal parts in this song?
10. Complete the following sentence:
    The structure of 'Defying Gravity' is based on ________ and ________ form.
11. Glinda and Elphaba sometimes sing in unison. What is meant by unison?
12. What does the sign (tremolo strokes) above or below a note indicate?
13. In musicals, woodwind players are often required to double. What does this mean?
14. The end of the song include parts for 'Ensemble'. What is another name for this group of singers?
15. What is the meaning of the 𝄐 symbol in the last few bars of the song?

Answers: See page 70

Set work 2

John Williams: 'Main Title' / 'Rebel Blockade Runner' (from *Star Wars: Episode IV – A New Hope*)

Context

Specially commissioned music for films first appeared in the 1930s. Many of the early composers in the genre had emigrated to Hollywood from Austria and eastern Europe, and continued to write for large symphony orchestras in the late Romantic style with which they were familiar. The 1950s saw the use of jazz in some film scores, and from the 1960s onwards film soundtracks included styles as diverse as pop, rock and experimental electronic music.

From the 1970s onwards, John Williams (born 1932) reinvigorated the style of the early film composers, producing highly successful film scores in a late Romantic idiom (spiced with occasional more modern dissonance) and designed for the rich resources of a full symphony orchestra.

Star Wars, released in 1977, was the first in what is now being developed into a cycle of nine related movies. It later received the sub-title '*Episode IV – A New Hope*' to indicate its position within the complete cycle. The films are set in a distant galaxy and concern an epic struggle between the evil Galactic Empire and the organised resistance of the Rebel Alliance, who are fighting to restore democracy.

Another traditional aspect of Williams' work is his use of **leitmotifs** – musical ideas associated with a character, object or event that are transformed to become grander, sadder, more romantic or whatever else the dramatic situation demands. The device was pioneered in the 19th-century operas of Richard Wagner.

In *Star Wars*, the motif starting on the upbeat to bar 4 of the set work is used to portray heroism and adventure, and soon becomes associated with the hero Luke Skywalker – in fact, just its opening notes are enough to suggest *Star Wars* to anyone who has seen the film:

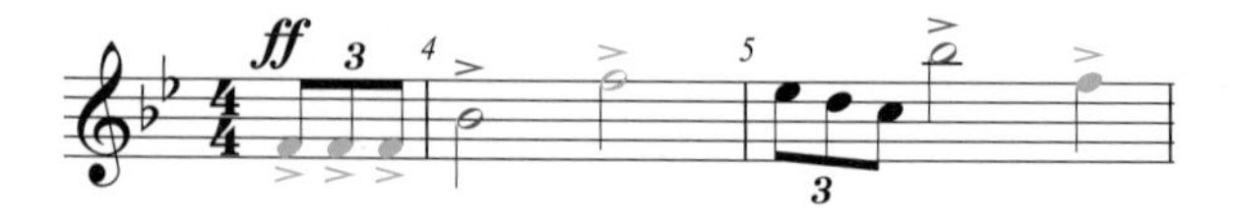

The motif gets its heroic quality from a loud dynamic, its scoring for trumpets and its focus on the two most important notes in the key of B♭ major – the tonic (B♭, shown in red) and the dominant (F, shown in blue). In addition, the motif starts with strong rising intervals and the triplet in bar 5, instead of falling a step to B♭, defiantly leaps a 7th to a high B♭. Triplets are often a feature of heroic music, and here they add to the march-like quality, while the syncopated accompaniment to these bars helps create the overall mood of excitement.

John Williams' transformations of this leitmotif occur later in the film in excerpts not included in the Anthology. For example, when Luke ponders his destiny, it is played thoughtfully and slowly by solo flute, then solo clarinet, accompanied by tremolo strings. When he rescues Leia (who turns out to be his twin sister) it becomes strongly rhythmic and percussive.

The main title of *A New Hope* is particularly important because the first half of this heroic music is the basis for the main title music in all of the Star Wars films, acting as an important unifying force for the series. Its continuation, though, is different in each film.

In the case of *A New Hope*, a second leitmotif is introduced in the final 10 bars of the set work. Known as the **Rebel Blockade Runner**, (or 'rebel fanfare') this is heard whenever the Rebel Alliance (or one of its spaceships) is trying to outrun the spaceships of the evil Empire. It is particularly like Wagner's leitmotifs in its brevity being, in essence, just an interval of a minor 3rd:

Resources

The music is scored for a full symphony orchestra of nearly 90 players:

- 10 woodwind, 11 brass, 6 percussion, harp and 60 strings (divided into five parts: first violins, second violins, violas, cellos and double basses)

The Anthology is printed as a **short score**, containing just three staves per line and showing only the most important orchestral parts.

Make sure you understand the abbreviations:

Trp.	Trumpet	***Hrp.***	Harp
Trb.	Trombone	***Vln.***	Violins
Hrn.	Horn	***Str.***	Strings
Timp.	Timpani	***Fl.***	Flutes

Tutti (e.g. in bar 21) means all, or everyone. The diagonal beams over the topmost notes in bars 1–6 and elsewhere indicate a tremolo for violins, played by small, very rapid movements of the bow across the strings.

The score for *A New Hope* was orchestrated by Herbert W. Spencer, who had long experience in scoring film musicals for Hollywood. The music is thickly scored, with much doubling of parts, few solo lines and no use of electric guitars, synthesisers or electronic effects.

Structure

The structure is largely determined by the visual images on screen that the music is designed to accompany. The first 29 bars consist of a short introductory fanfare followed by a ternary (ABA^1) structure, creating the familiar opening to all the *Star Wars* films. The second part sets the scene for this particular film, *A New Hope*:

Bars	Time	Music		Film
1–3^3	**0:00**	Introductory fanfare		The title 'Star Wars', fills the screen but immediately recedes into the distance
3^4–11^3	**0:07**	**A**	4-bar theme on trumpets, immediately repeated with a different accompaniment	Three paragraphs of scrolling text (the 'main title crawl'), each aligned to one of these three sections of music. They explain the background to the film.
11^4–20^3	**0:26**	**B**	8-bar contrasting theme on violins plus link (bar 20)	
20^4–29^3	**0:48**	**A^1**	Repeat of A, more fully scored with small changes and a link (bar 29)	

29^4–35	**1:09**	Shortened fanfare, crescendo and diminuendo	Tiny stars appear against the black void.
36^4–39^1	**1:25**	Piccolo solo, mysterious harmony	
39^2–50 51 - 60	**1.31** **1.56**	Sudden orchestral outburst followed by Rebel Blockade Runner leitmotif.	The surface of a huge planet swings into view. A tiny rebel spacecraft is being fired on by a spaceship of the Galactic Empire.

Tonality

The first half of the set work (up to bar 29) is in B♭ major, reinforced by an inverted tonic pedal on B♭ in bars 1–6, a dominant pedal on F in bars 11–14, and phrases that end with a dominant chord of F, creating imperfect cadences.

The music becomes increasingly **atonal** in the second half, with dissonant chords and a sense of **bitonality** in the last 10 bars, where chords in A♭ minor clash with a rhythmic **ostinato** on a pedal C.

Harmony

There is quartal harmony (chords built from 4ths) in the first seven bars.

Chords in root position, often with added notes, then predominate in the rest of the first section. There is some chromaticism, for example in the parallel triads of bar 7.

The unrelated chords in bars 33–35 create little sense of key, but the interval of an augmented 5th between A♭ and E♮ that permeates bars 32–39^1 gives the music a mystic, unworldly character, illustrating the void of space seen on screen at this point.

Chords become increasingly dissonant in the following bars, with A♭ clashing against triads of C major, until note **clusters** of C – D♭ – F – G are hammered out in bars 46–50. Parallel triads return in the last four bars, heard over a pedal C.

Melody

Bold, clearly-defined melodies are a feature of John Williams' style and are evident in the first section of the set work.

The intervals of a 4th and a 7th, and the triplet quaver rhythm, that were all prominent in the opening fanfare, also figure in the melody of section A:

A rising contour, based on the tonic (B♭) and dominant (F) of the key, helps to give this melody its heroic quality.

The main theme of the B section (bars 11⁴–19) forms a contrast, being scored for violins in octaves, having a less forceful dynamic and an elegant sweep with more stepwise movement, but it too makes reference to the intervals of a 4th and 7th, and to a quaver triplet rhythm:

Rhythm

The brisk tempo and $\frac{4}{4}$ time create a march-like military mood, and the triplet figures in the first three bars, scored for brass, are typical of fanfares.

The syncopated accompaniment in bars 4–6 and 21–24 adds to the excitement. The pulse becomes less obvious from bar 33, the time changes to triple metre at bar 44 and the music gradually slows in bars 47–50. The last 10 bars are at a faster tempo.

Texture

Mainly homophonic (melody and accompaniment, often with the melody doubled in octaves). A few imitative points (e.g. trumpets and trombones in opening fanfare). A **homorhythmic** texture of block chords in bars 44–50. Several pedal points, including a rhythmic **ostinato** on a pedal C in bars 51–end.

Test yourself

1. Describe ***two*** distinctive features of John Williams' film music.
2. How many bars long is the introductory fanfare in *Star Wars*?
3. Identify ***two*** aspects of the music in the openings bars that makes it sound like a fanfare.
4. The first section of music following the fanfare has an ABA[1] structure. Describe ***two*** similarities and ***two*** differences between sections A and B.
5. Explain the difference between bitonality and atonality by completing the following sentence:

   Bitonality is the use of ____ ,

   whereas atonality is ____ .
6. What is the meaning of:
   a. ***tutti*** (in bar 21)
   b. ***pizz.*** (in bar 33)
   c. ***8va*** (in bar 36)
7. Describe the texture in bars 44–50
8. Which ***two*** words describe the rhythm of the accompaniment in bars 21–24?
9. What is a cluster?

Answers: See page 70

AREA OF STUDY 4:

Fusions

Fusion is non-classical music that combines different styles - originally jazz and rock, but now almost any blend of contrasting musical traditions from around the world that merge to form something new.

Set work 1

Afro Celt Sound System: 'Release' (from the album *Volume 2: Release*)

Context and resources

The group Afro Celt Sound System was formed in 1995 and its second album, *Volume 2: Release*, appeared in 1999. The title track, *Release*, is the first song on the album. The name of the group reveals the origins of its own style of fusion:

- *Afro* - specifically the sounds of West African music, represented in this song by:
  - a **kora** (a type of harp)
  - a **djembe** (a goblet-shaped drum)
  - a **talking drum** (which can seem to mimic the tone patterns of speech)
- *Celt* - specifically the sounds of Irish traditional music, represented in this song by:
  - **uilleann pipes** (Irish bagpipes with softer tone than the Scottish variety)
  - a **fiddle** (the folk musician's name for a violin)
  - an **accordion** (that has hand-operated bellows which blow metal reeds)
  - a **low whistle** (an instrument like a metal recorder)
  - a **bodhrán** (a hand-held drum played with a double-headed beater)
  - a **hurdy-gurdy** (a mechanical violin in which the strings are made to vibrate by a wheel turned by a cranked handle and with strings that sound accompanying **drones**)
- *Sound System* - specifically the sounds and techniques of modern electronic dance music, including:

- male and female vocals
- synthesiser and samples
- electric piano, drum machine
- shaker and tambourine
- various digital effects.

The first voice heard on the track (at 0:41) is that of the West African kora player, N'Faly Kouyaté, who recites a softly spoken introduction in Maninka, one of the languages of Guinea. Verses 1 and 3 are sung in English by the famous Irish singer-songwriter Sinéad O'Connor, who also wrote the lyrics of the song. The male vocalist for verse 2 is Iarla Ó Lionáird, who sings in Irish (his words are not printed in the Anthology). The three languages symbolise the triple roots of Afro Celt Sound System's style.

Metre, tempo and rhythm

- The opening section is in **free time**
- Moderately fast tempo in $\frac{4}{4}$ time from 0:48 (where the loops start)
- Rhythm is slightly **swung**
- Rhythms in the vocal melodies include **syncopation**
- The instrumental solos, and some of the instrumental loops, feature strings of rapid short notes, echoing the fast decorative style of much Irish folk music
- Triplets feature in the low whistle solo and the fiddle loops.
- Repeating loops create the effect of **ostinatos** or **riffs**.
- The figure 4 above the final rest in loops 13, 17, 24, 26 and 28 indicates that the rest lasts for four-bars.

Tonality and harmony

- The tonality is best described as **modal**. Without B♮ (the leading note of C minor) it cannot be described as being in the key of C minor, but it is anchored to C by **drones** and by repeating patterns based on a chord of C minor.
- The music has a slow harmonic pace ('static harmony') and is mainly diatonic.

Texture

Mainly **homophonic**, with an accompaniment featuring a **layered texture** created from the 28 loops printed in the Anthology.

Structure

The song is based on three verses, preceded by an **intro**, concluded by an **outro**, and with instrumental sections described as 'solos' and 'drum break and build' in the Anthology score. There are no choruses. The accompaniment is constructed from loops, built up in layers, only the first entries of which are generally shown in the table below. Sections consist of mainly eight-bar phrases. The terms in brackets refer to music examples in the Anthology score.

0:00	**Intro**	Synth drone, with electronic effects, panned left and right. Talking drum + softly spoken introduction in Maninka. Percussion loops 1–3 then female introductory phrases (fig.1) with synth (loop 4) and drums (loop 5).
1:38	**Verse 1**	Female vocal sung in English (fig.2). Three similar stanzas (labelled 1, 2 and 3 in the Anthology) accompanied by loops 6–10. Voice stops at 2:35: short break formed by loops 11–13.
2:55	**Verse 2**	Male vocal sung in Irish (fig.3). Loop 14 enters. Vocal phrases are similar to those of verse 1 but gradually rise higher in pitch. Fig.4 starts at 3:14. **Double-stopped** pattern on fiddle (loop 15) enters very quietly and bass drops out until the end of section.
3.51	**Solos**	Uillean pipes solo (fig.5), later joined by whistle (octave higher). Synth (loop 16) and accordion (loop 17) join accompaniment. Low whistle solo (fig.6); bodhrán (loop 18) and synth strings (loop 10) are prominent in a generally lighter accompaniment. Hurdy-gurdy solo (loop 20) with synth pad (loop 21); talking drums, bodhrán and male vocal sample (loop 19) prominent in the mix.
4.55	**Verse 3**	Female vocal (repeat of fig. 2, stanzas 2 and 3 only), with synth (loop 22), while hurdy-gurdy and many other loops continue. Uilleann pipes (fig.5) added for stanza 3. Then male vocal (repeat of fig.4, second time only) with prominent fiddle part (loop 23); bass is silent; section ends with one bar of bodhrán and shaker.

5.51	**Build**	A long crescendo and thickening of texture. Drum break (loop 24) with bass (loop 12) and drum loops 1 and 2. Loops 25 and 26 (electric piano) added. Hurdy-gurdy (loop 27) replaces electric piano loops. Female vocalist adds isolated background notes (mainly on G, falling to C). Uilleann pipes (loop 28) added to mix.
6.59	**Outro**	Female vocal (repeat of fig. 2, stanza 3 - "Reach out and you'll touch me...") accompanied by drum, percussion, synth and fiddle loops (the last of which is particularly prominent in this section). Fade out, featuring electric piano loops 25 and 26.

Melody

- Mainly **modal** (Aeolian mode on C)
- Verse 1: just the 5 pitches of the **pentatonic minor** scale (C - E♭ - F - G - B♭)
- Repetitive: many **similar** two-bar phrases that fall from G to C
- Introductory vocal solo (fig.1) closely based on the falling melody of verse 1
- Male voice in verse 2 rises to a top C and has a wider range (a 10th, later extending to a 13th in loop 19)
- Vocal line has mainly **conjunct** movement (+ occasional small skips of a 3rd)
- Mostly **syllabic**, some parts spoken (whispered)
- Female vocal has a narrow **range** (6th) and low **tessitura**
- Some parts are **sampled**
- Use of **reverberation**
- Instrumental solos are more wide-ranging in pitch and include some disjunct movement, but they too emphasise G and C as the main notes of the mode.

Other points

A pad (in loops 4, 11 and 21) is a sustained synthesiser sound, often resembling strings, organ or voices. 'Vox' in loop 19 is Latin for voice, so 'male vox' means male vocalist.

The word 'pickup' in some of the loops shows where the loop starts - it indicates that the loop begins with an anacrusis.

Test yourself

1. Name ***two*** West African instruments that feature in the song *Release*.
2. Name ***two*** Irish folk instruments that feature in the song *Release*.
3. Name ***two*** electronic instruments that feature in the song *Release*.
4. What is meant by a loop in electronic dance music?
5. Explain the difference between the range and the tessitura of a vocal melody.
6. Describe the rhythm at the start of this song.
7. What is an outro?
8. Give an alternative technical term for each of the following:
   - a. **riff**
   - b. **drone**
   - c. **stepwise**
   - d. **Aeolian mode**
9. The first verse of *Release* is sung by Sinéad O'Connor. What other contribution did she make to this track?
10. The melody in the first stanza of *Release* uses a scale of five pitches. What is the name for a five-note scale?
11. In which language is the second verse of *Release*?
12. What is meant by a layered texture?
13. What type of sound is a pad?

Answers: See page 71

Set work 2

'Samba Em Prelúdio', performed by Esperanza Spalding (from the album *Esperanza*)

Context

Samba became popular during the 20th century as the national dance of Brazil, where its loud drumming and syncopated rhythms form an essential and exciting part of the carnival season. A more restrained version of samba is also known around the world as a competitive ballroom dance.

'Samba Em Prelúdio', written in 1962, is a **bossa nova**. Meaning 'new trend', it developed in the late 1950s as an alternative to the boisterous carnival samba. Bossa nova is slower and more lyrical than samba, with a focus on rich and complex harmonies borrowed from contemporary cool jazz. It became internationally famous when *The Girl from Ipanema*, a song by the Brazilian composer Antônio Carlos Jobim, became a hit in 1964.

'Samba Em Prelúdio' was composed by Roberto Baden Powell de Aquino (1937–2000), a virtuoso Brazilian guitarist and composer who had been encouraged to popularise *bossa nova* by Jobim. The title means 'Samba in the form of a prelude' (a prelude being a short piece written in the style of an improvisation).

The Portuguese lyrics, which were added after the music was composed, are by the Brazilian poet and playright, Vinícius de Moraes, who two years later would write the original Portuguese lyrics to 'The Girl from Ipanema' for Jobim. They tell a sad story of lost love (*saudade* in bars 24–25 refers to a feeling of deep longing or melancholy that some think characteristic of Brazilian temperament). Portuguese is the language of Brazil.

The Anthology recording of 'Samba Em Prelúdio' was released in 2008 as the last track on Esperanza Spalding's album *Esperanza*. Esperanza Spalding (born 1984) is an American singer and multi-instrumentalist, who plays acoustic bass guitar on this track, as well as singing the vocal line.

Resources

Female voice with a low tessitura (ranging from E below middle C upwards to G a 10th higher).

The **acoustic bass guitar** is a large version of the acoustic guitar. Its four strings are tuned to E, A, D and G (the same notes as the double bass and electric bass guitar). The part includes broken chords, scale patterns and **double stopping** (playing two notes at the same time) as well as ornaments such as the **mordent** in bar 1, the **harmonic** on the highest note in bar 3 and the **glissando** from the low F♯ that follows this note up towards D at the end of the bar.

An acoustic guitar joins the accompaniment in bar 23, where it plays chords and melodic fragments between the vocal phrases. The acoustic guitar also has a **virtuoso** solo in the middle of the song.

Structure

Note that at the end of bar 103 in the Anthology score, the direction D.S. al Coda (*Dal Segno al Coda*, meaning 'from the sign to the coda;) is an instruction to go back to the 𝄋 sign in bar 39 and repeat from there up to the end of bar 52, where the instruction 'to Coda 𝄌' indicates a jump on to the coda sign (𝄌) in bar 104.

The song includes two main melodies, labelled A and B in the table below. Each is immediately repeated in varied form (so the structure is AA¹ in bars 4–22 and BB¹ in bars 23–54). After a guitar solo in the middle of the song (bars 55–87) based on the chords of section B, the two melodies are heard together in counterpoint in bars 88–103.

Bars	Time	Section	Music
1–3	**0:00**	Intro	Solo in free tempo for acoustic bass guitar.
4–22	**0:16**	AA¹	Verse 1. 8 bars (bars 4–11) with varied repeat in bars 12–18. Introduction to Bossa nova indication begins in bar 19 (1:10).
23–54	**1:19**	BB¹	Verse 2 (different music). Acoustic guitar joins in. 16 bars (bars 23–38) with a varied repeat in bars 39–54.

55-87	**2:24**	Guitar solo	Guitar solo based on chords of section B. Only the first part of this solo (up to bar 69) is printed in the Anthology.
88-103	**3:35**	Repeats	Bass plays an **augmented** version of vocal melody A over which the voice sings verse 3 to a simplified version of melody B (bars 23-38). Acoustic guitar is silent. Followed by an exact repeat of B[1] (bars 39-52), which is indicated by *Dal Segno* (explained opposite).
104-114	**4:35**	Coda	Based on melody of bars 50-53, sung twice more.

The bass in bars 88-103 is an augmented version of the vocal melody in bars 4-11 (i.e. note lengths are increased - mostly doubled):

Texture

The texture in bars 1-3 is monophonic, apart from the two double stops.

Much of the rest of the song is **homophonic** (melody and accompaniment) although the combination of two independent melodic lines in bars 88-103 is **contrapuntal**.

Tonality

The music is in the key of B minor. There are no modulations although there are many chromatic notes.

Harmony

Many of the chords are complex because *bossa nova* is based on the rich harmonic vocabulary of cool jazz. Plain triads in root position are rare and when they do occur, non-chord notes are freely mixed in.

Chord extensions (7ths, 9ths, 11ths and 13ths) are used, along with chromatic chords such as the diminished 7th (e.g. in bars 33 and 35) and the chords of C and F (which are both chromatic in the key of B minor) in bars 27 and 28. Notice that both chords also include extensions and chromatic alterations, typical of cool jazz.

An extended chord (often an 11th) is frequently used to end a jazz performance. Here, the final chord is labelled Bm^{13} (it is actually $Bm^{\sharp 13}$ because the 13th is G♯). The B in the bass is the tonic, but it soon dies away leaving a shimmering discord containing the 3rd, 7th, 9th, 11th and ♯13th of the chord, deliberately avoiding any sense of finality.

Melody

The vocal melody in the A section is based on a four-note rising figure (shown in the first music example on page 53) that is varied throughout bars 4–17.

Each phrase spans a 7th (apart from the first, which spans a 6th) and the first or second note of each phrase falls by a step, creating a free, downward sequence. The falling sequence, low tessitura and minor key create a sad mood, designed to portray the melancholy lyrics. The melody in the A section moves mainly by leaps of between a 3rd and a 7th.

Melody B is almost entirely **conjunct**, with bars 31–34 being a repeat of bars 23–26 transposed up a 4th. Bars 34^3–36^2 are repeated in descending sequence to form bars 36^3–38^2.

The word setting throughout is syllabic.

The instrumental melodies have an improvisatory character. In the introduction the acoustic bass guitar part consists of **broken-chord** and scale-based figures. Notice how the unaccompanied pattern in bar 2 returns in bar 7, and is changed to a triplet rhythm in bar 15. The acoustic guitar solo in bars 55–87 is again based on scale and chord patterns, and shows the range and versatility of the instrument in its upper register. Note the guitarist's use of fingered **tremolo** at 2:53 and 3:25.

Metre, tempo and rhythm

The song is in simple quadruple time. The $\frac{5}{4}$ in bar 3 is just a way of expressing the free rhythm of the opening rather than a distinct change in metre. These first three bars have a thoughtful, improvisatory quality achieved through rubato – tiny fluctuations in tempo for expressive effect. There is not a strict sense of pulse in this opening, hence the direction 'Free tempo' in bar 1.

Because much of the musical detail is improvised, the transcription into notation inevitably makes the rhythm look complex with the frequent use of triplets and syncopation.

Another important rhythmic feature of *Samba em prelúdio* is the use of **cross rhythm**. This is when two rhythmic patterns that conflict with each other occur simultaneously:

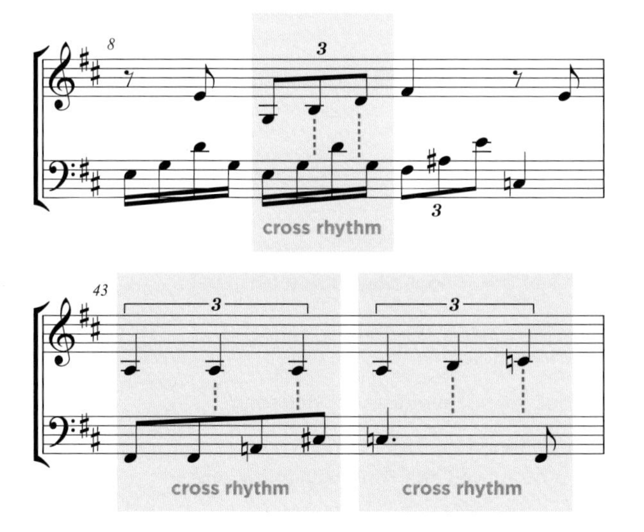

The direction 'Bossa nova (in tempo)' in bar 19 marks the start of the dance section of the song, with the *bossa nova*'s characteristic combination of gently syncopated and dotted rhythms.

Test yourself

1. What is the meaning of bossa nova?
2. Name ***two*** ways in which bossa nova differs from samba.
3. In what language are the lyrics of 'Samba Em Prelúdio'?
4. Compare the acoustic bass guitar with an electric bass guitar by naming ***one*** similarity and ***one*** difference.
5. What does it mean to describe the guitar solo in the middle of 'Samba Em Prelúdio' as virtuoso?
6. What is a coda?
7. Complete the gaps in the following:

   Dal segno al coda is an instruction to ________________ the music from the 𝄋 sign until the words 'to coda' and then ________________ to the 𝄌 sign for the coda.
8. What is another term for a coda?
9. Complete the following sentence:
   When a rhythm is augmented its notes become ________________ .
10. The highest note in bar 3 of the song is played as a harmonic. What is a harmonic?
11. In what key is 'Samba Em Prelúdio'?
12. What do you notice about the vocal register of this song?
13. Complete the following sentence:
    'Samba Em Prelúdio' is a fusion of Latin American music and ____________ .
14. What name is given to chords such as C^9, Bm^{11} and Bm^{13}?

Answers: See page 71

The elements of music

The following elements are the building blocks of every type of music – be it folk, pop, rock, jazz, classical or world music.

Because it is often necessary to refer to these elements in exams, you may find it helpful to remember **DR T SMITH**:

Dynamics
Rhythm (including metre and tempo)
Texture
Structure
Melody
Instrumentation (including voices or other resources)
Tonality
Harmony

Below are some of the things that could be discussed within each element.

Dynamics

Dynamics are the relative levels of quietness or loudness in music:

quieter →					louder
pianissimo	*piano*	*mezzo-piano*	*mezzo-forte*	*forte*	*fortissimo*
pp	***p***	***mp***	***mf***	***f***	***ff***

Dynamics also include *crescendo* or *cresc.* (gradually get louder), *diminuendo* or *dim.* (gradually get quieter), and accents (extra emphasis given to some notes).

Just listing the dynamics in a piece will not gain marks. It is important to show how the dynamics are used. For example:

- Are changes to the dynamics frequent, sudden or gradual?
- Does a *crescendo* lead to a climax?
- Is a *diminuendo* used to make the music fade away at the end?
- Are different dynamic levels used to create contrasts, as in the **terraced dynamics** of much Baroque music?
- Are some notes accented for special emphasis?

Rhythm (including tempo and metre)

As with dynamics, aim to show how rhythm contributes to the effect of the music:

- Do the rhythms use solemn long notes or energetic short notes?
- Are there characteristic patterns such as particular dance rhythms, dotted rhythms, swing rhythms or triplets?
- Are rests an important feature in the main rhythmic patterns?
- Is there any syncopation?

Tempo is the speed of the beat or pulse. This may be indicated by an Italian word such as:

lento	very slow
adagio	slow
largo	broadly (quite slow)
andante	walking pace (not too slow)
allegretto	a little brisk

moderato	moderately
allegro moderato	moderately fast
allegro	fast, joyful
vivace	lively
presto	very quick

Alternatively, tempo can be shown by the number of beats per minute, such as 60 bpm or ♩=60 (indicating 60 beats per minute, which is a slow pace of one beat per second).

It is usually relevant to mention any change in tempo, such as:

- A ***ritardando*** (***rit.***), ***rallentando*** (***rall.***) or ***allargando*** – a gradual slowing down, often to mark the end of a piece or section
- An ***accelerando*** (***accel.***) – a gradual speeding up, often to create excitement
- A pause (shown by 𝄐 over a note), perhaps used for dramatic effect.

A performance might include ***rubato*** – fluctuations in tempo for expressive effect. The direction 'free time' indicates music in which the rhythm does not have to fit a regular pulse. Similarly, the Italian ***colla voce*** ('with the voice') is a direction that an accompaniment should follow the rhythm of the singer.

If the speed doesn't vary, don't ignore the obvious – point out that the tempo is unchanging.

Metre is the pattern of beats in a piece of music. In duple metre there are two main beats per bar (strong-weak), in triple metre there are three (strong-weak-weak), and in quadruple metre there are four (strong-weak-weak-weak).

- If the upper figure of the time signature is 2, 3 or 4 the metre is **simple**: each beat can be split into two shorter notes of identical length

- If the upper figure of the time signature is 6, 9 or 12 the metre is **compound**: each beat can be split into three shorter notes of identical length.

2 beats per bar	$\frac{2}{4}$ = simple duple metre	$\frac{6}{8}$ = compound duple metre
3 beats per bar	$\frac{3}{4}$ = simple triple metre	$\frac{9}{8}$ = compound triple metre
4 beats per bar	$\frac{4}{4}$ = simple quadruple metre	$\frac{12}{8}$ = compound quadruple metre

Any change of metre in a piece deserves comment, as does any unusual metrical effect (such as a $\frac{6}{8}$ melody accompanied by a bass part in $\frac{3}{4}$ time). A **cross rhythm** occurs when two conflicting rhythms are heard together (such as two quavers against a triplet of three quavers). If there is no clear beat, we say that there is no regular metre or that the music has a free rhythm.

Texture

Texture refers to the way that the various simultaneous lines in a piece relate to one another. The three main types of texture are:

Monophonic An unaccompanied melody

If the music is monophonic, is it performed by just one person or by a number of people who all play or sing the same tune in **unison** or in **octaves**?

Homophonic An accompanied melody

If the accompaniment is reasonably independent of the tune the texture is **melody and accompaniment**. If the tune and accompaniment mainly move together in the same rhythm the texture is **chordal**.

Polyphonic Two or more simultaneous melodies

Also known as a **contrapuntal** texture (a texture consisting of **counterpoint**). If the music is polyphonic, is there **imitation**? If the imitation is exact the texture may be **canonic**. How many independent lines are there? For example, three-part counterpoint would have three independent lines of music. Melodic lines in counterpoint are called 'voices' even if they are played rather than sung.

Other types of texture include:

- **Heterophonic**, in which different versions of a melody are heard at the same time
- **Antiphonal**, in which two or more spatially separated soloists or groups perform alternately and in combination.
- A **layered texture**, in which repetitive patterns drop in and out of the overall texture to provide areas of contrast (as occurs in minimalist music and in some types of music from Africa and other world cultures)
- A **fugal** texture (or **fugato**), in which a short melodic idea is introduced at different pitches by each part in turn, imitating and overlapping with the previous parts, which each continue in counterpoint with the new part.

Remember that texture often changes during the course of a piece and that other features of the music may have an impact on the texture, such as an **ostinato**, **pedal**, **countermelody** or **dialogue** between different instruments.

Edexcel advises against using vague terms such as 'thick texture' or 'thin texture'. It is better to be more precise and use descriptions such as 'two-part counterpoint' or 'texture of four-part chords'.

Structure

Structure may refer to the overall plan of a composition, such as ternary form, sonata form or verse and chorus. The overall form is sometimes expressed in capital letters, such as ABA for ternary form (or ABA^1 if there are differences in the A section when it is repeated). If you do use letters to identify passages in the music, be sure to explain which part of the music each letter refers to.

Structure can also refer to the way in which individual phrases relate to each other and are constructed from short motifs. Are the phrases paired in a question-and-answer (or call-and-response) style – known as balanced or **periodic phrasing**?

Try to show the purpose of the various sections – for instance, a **fanfare** might announce the start of a piece, the **exposition** in sonata form introduces the main keys and themes, the **coda** is a concluding section intended to confirm the tonic key, and an **instrumental** in a song adds variety and gives the singer a break.

Key elements to identify in the structure of music are repetition, contrast and varied repetition (which may be anything from a slightly changed ending to variation of an entire passage).

Melody

There are many questions to ask yourself when considering melody:

- Is the melody **diatonic**, **chromatic**, **pentatonic** or **modal**?
- Does it move mainly by step (**conjunct** movement) or by leap (**disjunct** movement), or does it include both types of movement?
- Is the melody smooth or angular in outline?
- Does it have a narrow or a wide range, and is it in a high or low **tessitura** (i.e. is it high or low in the range of the instrument or voice concerned)?
- Does it transfer from one instrument or voice to another?
- Is the melody decorated with lots of ornamental notes, or devices such as **glissando** and **pitch bend**, or is it plain and simple?
- How is the melody constructed? Is it formed from motifs that are repeated, or used in ascending or descending sequence, or does it unfold as a continuous line? Are there any prominent intervals, such as rising 5ths or diminished 7ths? Is there a clear climax, on a top note for example?
- Is the melody based on scale patterns or **triads**? Is it lyrical or fragmented? Does it have an overall shape - rising, falling or arch-like - or is it largely on a **monotone** (notes of the same pitch)? Are the main melodies in the piece contrasted with one another or are they similar?
- How is the melody articulated - is it mostly **legato** (smooth) or **staccato** (detached) and are some notes strongly accented?
- Is the melody an important theme on which part or all of the work is based?

Instrumentation (including voices and other resources)

Instrumentation, sometimes referred to as the resources (or forces) used in a composition, means not only the instruments, and/or voices employed but also the ways in which they are used.

You may need to identify these in general terms, such as a large orchestra (symphony orchestra) or small orchestra (chamber orchestra), or you may need to be more specific, such as identifying the group as a string orchestra, brass band or wind band (the last of these consisting of brass, woodwind and percussion).

Smaller ensembles include groups such as a brass quintet, string quartet (two violins, viola and cello), piano trio (violin, cello and piano), percussion ensemble and rock group. Jazz bands vary in size, but most include a horn section of saxophones, trumpet(s) and trombone(s) plus a rhythm section of piano, drums, guitar (or banjo), and either a plucked upright bass (i.e. a double bass) or bass guitar.

Most Baroque music for three or more players includes a **continuo** part, which would be played by a bass instrument and be used as the basis for improvising accompanying harmonies on a chordal instrument such as a harpsichord, organ or lute. There are often figures and other symbols below the notes in the continuo part to indicate the chords required (hence the term **figured bass**).

It is more important to show how instruments and/or voices are used rather than to just list them. For example, which instruments have solos, which accompany, how different combinations of instruments are used for contrast, which instruments **double** one another (either in **unison** or in **octaves**), which exchange ideas in **dialogue** with each other, and so forth.

An important ingredient in the **sonority** (tone colour) of music is the variety of **timbre** used. Timbre can refer to the sound produced by families of instruments (strings, woodwind or brass, for example), or to the tone quality of specific instruments. For example, the clarinet has a different timbre to the trumpet. Many instruments produce a different timbre in different parts of their range. For instance, the lower register of the clarinet is often described as hollow, dark, or 'oily' in character while its top register can sound brilliant, or even shrill when played very loudly.

Timbre can also be changed by the way an instrument is played, for example by using a **mute**, by plucking a string instead of using the bow, or by strumming a guitar rather than finger-picking its individual strings.

It may be relevant to discuss whether the music uses most of the available range on an instrument, or just part of it, and if any special effects, such as **tremolo** or **glissando**, are used. In pop and jazz, it may be appropriate to use terms such as brass **stabs** and drum **fills**, and to explain the use of electronic instruments, such as synthesisers, samplers or drum machines. You may need to point out the use of **effects** (such as **flanging** or **overdrive**) or to explain how the music is built up using **multi-tracking** or **overdubbing**.

Indicate the role of the singers in vocal music, either as soloists, choir or backing group. If there is a choir, does it consist of male voices, female voices or mixed voices? How many voice parts are there? Music for choirs (choral music) typically has four voice parts (soprano, alto, tenor and bass, abbreviated as SATB).

If vocal music is unaccompanied it may be described as **a capella**. If it is accompanied, do the instruments mainly double the voices or do they have largely independent parts? Do the vocal parts have a wide range or are they mainly in a high or low **tessitura**? Is the word-setting **syllabic**, **melismatic** or a mixture of both? Is there any obvious **word-painting**?

Tonality

Tonality is about the use of major and/or minor keys in music, and the ways in which such keys are related. Be careful not to make the common mistake of imagining that it is about the tone colours of music. Issues include:

- Is the music major, minor, modal or atonal?
- Does it modulate? If so, are the modulations to related or unrelated keys?
- Are any modulations in the music sudden or are they prepared for?
- Is the music mainly **diatonic** or are there **chromatic** sections?
- Does the use of different keys help define the structure of the music?

Don't assume that minor keys are sad and major keys are happy. A fast minor-key movement can sound energetic or angry, just as a slow piece in a major key can sound tragic (for example, the famous march from Handel's *Saul*, played at most state funerals, is in C *major*).

Harmony

Issues to consider include:

- The main type of chords used: are they mainly primary triads, perhaps in root position, or are there 7ths and extended chords (9ths, 11ths and 13ths)?
- Is there a preponderance of major (or minor) chords? Remember that major chords occur in minor keys and that minor chords occur in major keys
- Is the harmony mainly **diatonic** or is it sometimes **chromatic**?
- Does the harmony occur in block chords or in **arpeggios** and **broken chords**?
- How **dissonance** is treated – is it used expressively through **appoggiaturas** and **suspensions**, or is it used freely for its own effect?
- Any **pedal** notes that underpin the harmony
- The rate at which chords change (the **harmonic pace**)
- The use of special effects, such as **parallel harmonies**
- The use of progressions such as the **circle of 5ths**
- Any particularly important **cadences**.

The listening paper

The exam for Component 3, Appraising, commonly called the listening paper, has two sections, A and B. In Section A (which is worth 68 marks) a relevant extract of music will be played on CD several times for each question.

Section A contains:

- Questions about musical features of six of the eight set works, most of which will require short answers
- A dictation question in which you have to add a few missing pitches, rhythms or chords to a stave of music
- A set of questions on a piece of unfamiliar music (it will be related to a set work and there will be a skeleton score of the music in the exam paper).

Section B is worth 12 marks and contains just one essay question:

- You will be asked to compare an extract from one of the set works with an extract from an unfamiliar piece (related to one of the set works).

Scores of both extracts for Section B will be printed in a 'Source Booklet' that accompanies the exam paper. You are likely to hear a recording of the familiar extract from a set work played once and the unfamiliar extract played several times before you start writing.

Section A

Use the reading time before the first music extract is played to check that you understand all of the questions. Underline any key words. Remember that in the heat of the moment it is easy to forget the meaning of technical terms such as texture and tonality.

Also look out for any questions you can answer without listening to the music - things such as naming the genre of one of the set works or stating what is meant by the continuo. Obviously, check your answer when you hear the recording, but getting these questions out of the way will allow you to concentrate on the other questions while the music is played.

On the exam paper, the mark available for each sub-question is shown in brackets. These marks should help you decide how long to spend on that part of the question as well as how many separate points to give in your answer. It is not worth spending a lot of time puzzling over a question worth only one mark if that is done at the expense of having to rush a question carrying three or four marks.

In questions that require several answers, such as naming three ways in which the music creates a sense of excitement, be precise and make sure your points are distinct as you won't get marks for making the same point again in different words. Vague statements such as saying that the music is exciting because it 'builds up' and is 'thrilling' are unlikely to get marks. You need to make three precise points, using technical terms, such as saying that the texture thickens as instruments are added, the dynamics increase in a long *crescendo* and note lengths get shorter and shorter.

It is important to work through sample questions before taking the exam, so that you get fully used to the language used in questions. In particular, note that:

- Questions asking you to identify a genre, period or interval, mean that you should give its name
- Questions asking you to identify similarities or differences mean that you should name or describe elements that are similar or different
- Questions asking you to name a device should be answered with the correct technical term (e.g. a melodic device might be a sequence)
- Questions about performance techniques are likely to refer to things such as using falsetto, glissando, harmonics, pitch bend and so forth
- Questions asking how a mood is achieved require precise answers using technical terms (see the example above about how excitement is created)
- Questions asking you to evaluate something (such as the suitability of a set work's title) require you to express opinions and draw conclusions

For some questions you will be asked to show your answer by drawing a cross in a box (☒) next to one of the alternatives in a list of choices. If you draw a cross in more than one box in the list, you will not receive a mark. If you change your mind about the answer, follow the instructions on the paper for indicating your incorrect choice (usually by drawing a line through the cross, like this ☒).

Section B

The single question in this section will require you to compare a passage from a set work with a piece of unfamiliar music. It needs a longer answer than anything in Section A, and should be written as a short essay – not as a list of bullet points.

Spend a few minutes planning what to include and check that you haven't forgotten anything before writing up your final answer. Devote a new paragraph to each point or group of points and leave a blank line or two after each paragraph, so that if you think of something to add later, it doesn't have to be too squashed-up.

Aim for clear English, with correct spelling and punctuation. For a top mark you must use music terminology correctly, and give examples of what you say by referring to precise locations in the score. Unless you are asked for a personal opinion, avoid using 'I' in this type of technical writing. It is best to refer to 'the melody' or 'the harmony' rather than using expressions such as 'I think' or 'I like'.

Top revision tips

1. Start revising as soon as you can - in the Christmas holiday if possible, otherwise no later than the start of the Easter break. Don't forget that your teacher may not be available to answer any questions you might have once revision leave has started, so begin revising early!
2. Draw up a plan, giving priority to the set works and topics that you feel least confident about. You could, if you wish, make copies of the blank table on page 68 to fill in for each week of your revision. It is best not to spend more than 10–20 minutes at a time on any one subject and it is important to include breaks in which you can switch off for a few minutes.
3. Avoid prevaricating - it will not help to spend hours decorating, colouring and laminating your revision timetable. You need to make an early start on revision and not keep finding excuses to put it off.
4. Don't try to revise by just staring at your notes as you won't take anything in. Instead, have a clear plan for each revision session, using the strategies listed below. Vary your routine by occasionally revising with classmates so that you can test each other as you go.
5. Start by summarising your notes on each set work, checking facts as you go. You may find it useful to write key points about each piece on record cards:

Beethoven Pathétique (1st Movement), 1799
- Classical (anticipates Romantic style)
- Sonata form (with introduction)
- Exposition / development / recapitulation
- Cm→E♭/Gm→Em→D→Gm/Cm→Cm
- Homophonic texture
- Periodic phrasing
- Melody based on small cells

Remember that understanding technical terms and using terms correctly in your answers is especially important. Make sure that you know *precisely* what each term means. A sequence, for example, is not just an idea that is repeated at a different pitch. It has to be repeated *immediately* at a different pitch. An ostinato is not just a repeated pattern, it is a pattern repeated *many times in succession.*

6. Listen to each set work as often as possible. As you listen, make sure you can hear each of the key points you have listed and that you can identify the main instruments and/or voices in the piece. Try to retain the sound of the music in your head so that you can replay it in your imagination.
7. Never listen to music when revising, except the set work on which you are focusing. Anything else will be totally distracting. Put your mobile away when revising and avoid distractions such as the TV or the internet.
8. Test yourself using the questions in this book and the study guide, if you have a copy. Make a note of any points that look like they need further attention.
9. Check that you understand all of the terms in the glossary of this book. Make sure that you can think of at least one example of each of them from the set works. Again, this is information you could note on record cards if it helps.
10. Listen to a 30-second extract from each set work without following the score and write a comment about as many elements as you can in that time (e.g. contrapuntal texture, dotted rhythms, modulates to the dominant, florid harpsichord part). Check your answers against your notes and the comments in this revision guide.
11. Another good way to revise is in 10 minute sessions, each followed by a short test completed without looking at your notes. Test yourself again an hour later, then the next day, then after a week and again after a fortnight to see what has stuck and what has been forgotten.
12. Work through as many exam papers as you can, paying particular attention to the dictation questions and the extended answers required for Section B, which should each be worked under timed conditions of about 30 minutes.

One type of revision that rarely works is last-minute cramming, especially if done late on the night before the exam. Your brain needs time to reflect on concepts if they are to stick in your memory. You will do much better to have an early night and a good breakfast so that you can arrive fresh and on time for the exam, free of any panic about being late.

Failing to plan = Planning to fail

Using your time for effective revision means prioritising exam work in the final months of the course. This means limiting the time you spend online, on social media and playing computer games. Remember, it is only for a few months - but a few months that could make a difference to the rest of your life - after which your social life can resume and the partying continue!

It's not the hours you put in. It's what you put in to the hours that matters!

Good luck with your exams!

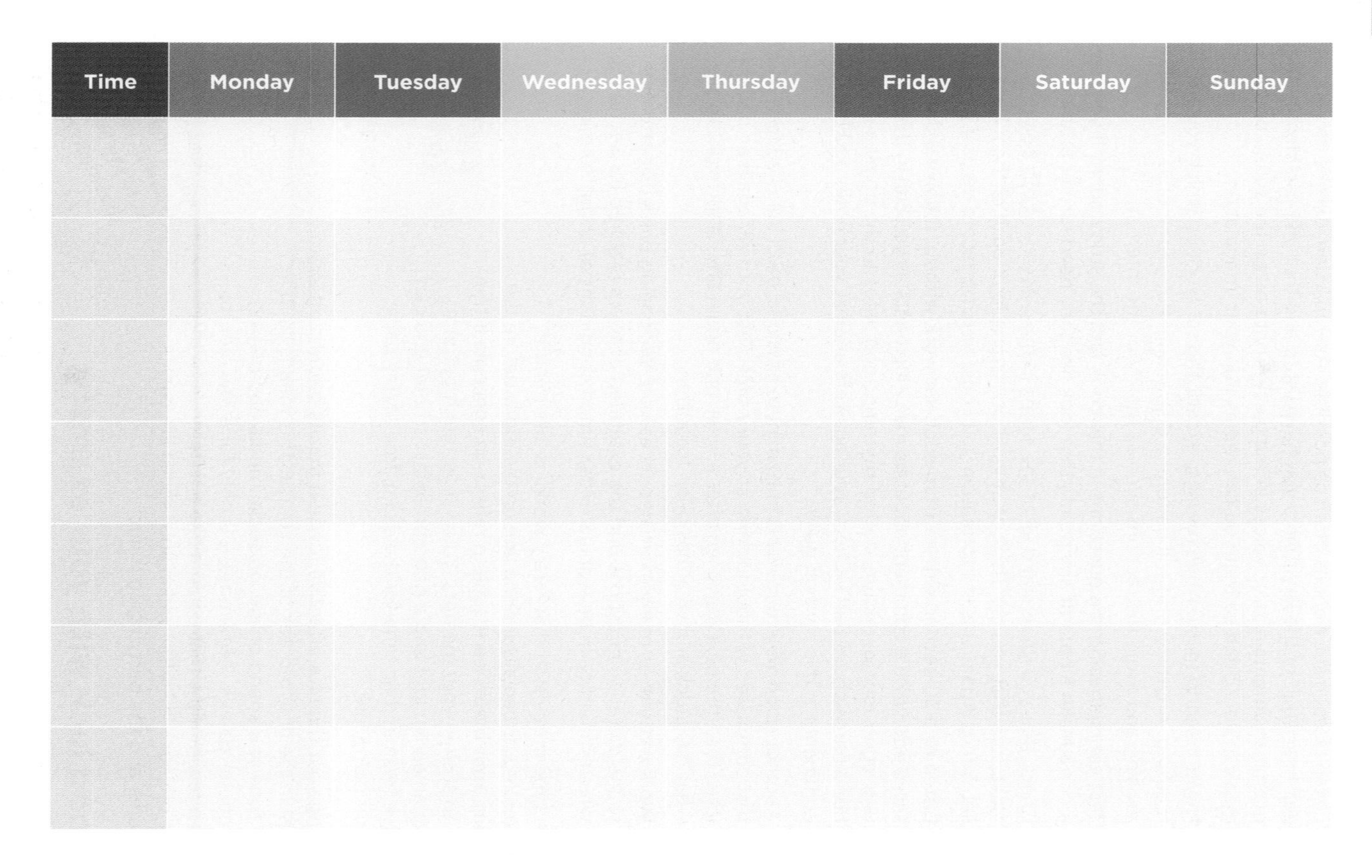

Time	Monday	Tuesday	Wednesday	Thursday	Friday	Saturday	Sunday

Answers

Words in brackets are optional. Alternative answers are separated by a slash (/). Other responses that answer the question posed may receive credit if they are accurate and unambiguous. However, for top marks you need to show that you can use and understand musical terminology.

AREA OF STUDY 1:

Set work 1 p10

1. Baroque
2. Concerto grosso
3. Flute, violin, harpsichord / cembalo
4. The orchestra / the accompanying parts
5. Fast speed, compound time / triplets
6. Bass: cello / double bass / violone / bassoon
   Chordal: Harpsichord / organ / lute
7. Improvising an accompaniment using chords based on the given figures
8. a. Structure: ternary form
   b. Texture: contrapuntal / polyphonic
9. B minor
10. Dominant
11. Stretto
12. Trill and appoggiatura
13. Belonging to the current key
14. Immediate

Set work 2 p19

1. Baroque, Classical, Romantic *(answer must be in this order)*
2. Vienna
3. Any two from: Haydn, Mozart, Schubert
4. Its music returns later in the movement
5. a. Transition / bridge passage
   b. Codetta
   c. Recapitulation
6. a. A passage that creates expectation for the return of the tonic key
   b. At the end of the development / just before the recapitulation
7. Accented / emphasised
8. Diminished 7th / augmented 6th
9. a. E♭ minor
   b. F minor
10. As short as possible

AREA OF STUDY 2:

Set work 1 p25

1. String
2. 17th
3. Ternary
4. Different lengths of ground bass and rapid modulations
5. Syllabic and melismatic
6. (Rising) sequence
7. Any two of: mordents, appoggiaturas, slides, grace notes, trills, arpeggiation
8. Any three of:
   ground bass suggests spirit of Laius rising, many repetitions of 'all' implies a multitude, melismas illustrate thoughtful 'wond'ring',

harsh discord on 'pains', resolving suspensions on the word 'eased', ascending phrase and major key for 'free the dead', long melismas winding around the same few notes to portray 'eternal', off-beat repetitions of 'drop' to suggest snakes dropping from Alecto's head.

9. Suspension
10. Music for performance as part of a play
11. G♯ (bass stave) and G♮ (treble stave)
    NB treble G♯s are not false relations as they are in the same part as the G♮

Set work 2 p32

1. Any one of: *Bohemian Rhapsody, We Will Rock You, We Are The Champions*
   (many other possibilities)
2. Bass guitar
3. Note(s) before the first strong beat of a phrase / an up-beat / a pick-up
4. Four
5. (Half-)spoken
6. Portamento / glissando
7. Small, rapid fluctuations in pitch to warm the tone of a note
8. Falsetto
9. Circle of 5ths
10. Nonsense syllables in a song
11. The notes of the chords all move in the same direction

AREA OF STUDY 3:

Set work 1 p39

1. Underscore / melodrama
2. a. Follow the rhythm of the singer
   b. Gradually slow down
3. Stabs / detached, accented chords
4. Music that mimics the rhythms of speech
5. (Ascending) (free) sequence
6. (Half-)spoken
7. Distortion
8. A pattern repeated many times in succession
9. Just under two octaves
10. Verse (and) chorus (form)
11. They sing the same notes
12. Continually and rapidly repeat the printed pitch for the length of the printed note / tremolo
13. Play more than one instrument
14. Chorus
15. Pause / hold the note for longer than usual

Set work 2 p45

1. Any two of:
   large symphony orchestra, Romantic style, leitmotifs, memorable melodies
2. 3
3. Any two of: use of trumpets / brass, triplets, rising intervals, march-like tempo, melody based on tonic and dominant
4. **Similarities**, any two of:
   both melodies include triplets, both melodies include prominent intervals of a 4th and a 7th, both include chromatic harmonies.

Differences, any two of:
B is softer than A, A features brass while B features strings / violins, the melody of B is more flowing, B has a smoother accompaniment.

5. Two keys at the same time; the lack of a sense of key or mode
6. a. Everyone / full orchestra
   b. Pluck (the strings)
   c. (Play) an octave higher (than written)
7. Homorhythmic / chordal
8. Any two of: syncopated, accented, triplets, detached
9. A dissonant chord that includes several notes only one step apart

AREA OF STUDY 4:

Set work 1 p50

1. Any two of: kora, djembe, talking drum
2. Any two of: uilleann pipes, bodhrán, fiddle, hurdy-gurdy, accordion, low whistle
3. Any two of: synthesiser, electric piano, drum machine, sampler
4. A short section of music that is continually repeated
5. Range is the span from lowest to highest note, tessitura is where in the range the music mainly lies
6. Free time / no clear pulse
7. Closing section / coda
8. a. Ostinato
   b. Pedal
   c. Conjunct
   d. Natural minor
9. She wrote the lyrics
10. Pentatonic
11. Irish
12. A texture formed from different types of repeating patterns
13. A sustained synthesiser timbre

Set work 2 p56

1. New trend
2. Any two of: more lyrical than samba, slower than samba, harmonies more complex / borrowed from jazz
3. Portuguese
4. **Similarity**: strings tuned to same notes / they have the same range
   Difference: electric bass is amplified
5. It is technically very difficult / very showy / it requires a highly skilled player
6. A closing section
7. Repeat; jump
8. Outro
9. Longer / twice as long
10. A very high note produced by stopping a string very lightly before plucking or bowing
11. B minor
12. It is very low
13. (Cool) jazz
14. Extended

Glossary

A cappella. Unaccompanied singing.

Acciaccatura. (pronounced *atch-akka-too-ra*). An **ornament**, printed as a small note with a slash through its tail, that is performed as quickly as possible on or just before the beat that follows it.

Accordion. An instrument with hand-operated bellows that force air to vibrate metal reeds. The sound is controlled from small buttons on both sides of the bellows, although the larger piano accordion has a small vertical keyboard on one side. An instrument often used in folk music.

Aeolian mode. A scale that can be found by playing the white notes on the piano from A to A an octave higher. It is the same as C major except that the home note is A. The mode can be transposed to start on any note providing that the order of tones and semitones in its scale is retained.

Alla breve. A pulse of two minim beats in a bar ($\frac{2}{2}$ time). Sometimes called cut-C time after its alternative time signature of 𝄵.

Alto. The lowest female singing voice. See also **countertenor**.

Anacrusis. One or more notes that occur before the first strong beat of a phrase (i.e. before the first bar line of the phrase). Often called a 'pick up' in jazz and pop music.

Antiphonal. A texture in which two or more spatially separated soloists or groups perform alternately and in combination.

Appoggiatura. (pronounced *a-podge-a-too-ra*). An expressive dissonance that then usually moves by step to a note of the current chord. If written as an **ornament**, the note forming the appoggiatura is printed in small type.

Aria. A song for solo voice with accompaniment, usually forming part of a longer work such as an **opera**, **oratorio** or **cantata**. See also **obbligato aria**.

Arpeggio. See **chord**.

Atonal. Western music that is not in a **key** or a **mode** and that is often **dissonant**.

Augment. **1**. A proportionate increase in note lengths, e.g. when a rhythm of two quavers and a crotchet is augmented it becomes two crotchets and a minim.
2. An augmented interval is a semitone larger than a major or a perfect interval. Augmentation is the opposite of **diminution**.

Backbeat. A term used in pop and rock to describe accenting the normally weak second and fourth beats in $\frac{4}{4}$ time.

Backing vocals. The vocal accompaniment to the **lead vocal** in a pop song. The part is often labelled BVOX.

Ballad. In jazz and pop, a slow, romantic song.

Baroque. In music, the period between about 1600 and 1750.

Bass. **1**. The lowest male singing voice. **2**. An abbreviation of double bass.

Bass guitar. A guitar that has the same pitch and tuning as a double bass and, also like the double bass, that sounds an octave lower than its written notes. Usually electrically amplified, it forms the harmonic foundation of a rock group by playing the bass line.

Basso continuo. See **continuo**.

Bass viol. A bowed string instrument of the viol family, similar in size to the later cello, but having between five and seven strings and a fretted fingerboard (like a guitar). See also **violone**.

Bell chord. A chord that is sounded as a downward succession of sustained notes.

Bend. A slight change in the pitch of a note while it is sounding. The change is usually upward and is made for expressive purposes.

Bitonal. Music in which two distinctly different keys occur simultaneously.

Bodhrán. A hand-held drum played with a double-headed tipper, used in much Irish traditional music.

Book. A document containing the spoken dialogue of a stage **musical**. See also **libretto**.

Book musical. A **musical** in which songs, vocal ensembles and dances are fully integrated into a plot with serious dramatic goals.

Bossa nova. A dance and highly syncopated style of music that developed in the 1960s. It is slower and gentler than **samba**, from which it developed, and the music was influence by jazz of the period.

Bouzouki. A plucked string instrument of the lute family usually associated with the music of Greece, but used by a number of Celtic folk musicians in recent decades.

Break. In pop and jazz, an instrumental solo (usually improvised), e.g. a saxophone break.

Breakbeat. A short section (often just one bar) of a dance track in which most instruments other than drums stop playing. The term is also used for a type of electronic dance music.

Breakdown. The section of a dance track in which sounds drop out prior to a **build**.

Bridge. A short and often contrasting passage in a pop song that links two other sections. Sometimes called a middle eight, even if not eight bars in length.

Broken chord. See **chord**.

Broken octaves. Rapidly alternating notes that are an **octave** apart.

Build. An abbreviation of build up. A term used mainly in electronic dance music for a long crescendo and thickening of texture. See also **breakdown**.

BVOX. See **backing vocals**.

Cadence. The end of a musical phrase, often harmonised by two chords. See **Imperfect cadence**, **Interrupted cadence**, **Perfect cadence**, **Plagal cadence**.

Cadenza. **1**. An improvised vocal flourish just before a singer's final **cadence** in an **aria**. **2**. In music from the Classical period onwards, an improvised or written out solo towards the end of a **movement** in a **concerto**, when the soloist plays alone to demonstrate their **virtuosity**.

Canon. A **contrapuntal** device in which the melody in one part is overlapped by the same melody in another part, starting a few notes later. This process of exact **imitation** continues throughout the length of the canon or canonic passage.

Chamber orchestra. A small orchestra, typically consisting of a small but complete string section plus a limited number of wind players.

Chord. Three or more pitches sounded simultaneously, although just two notes can often imply a chord by their context. In a broken chord or arpeggio, the notes are sounded separately but in close proximity to each other. See also **diminished 7th (2)**, **dominant 7th chord**, **triad**.

Chordal. A **homophonic** texture that consists mainly of block chords. Also known as **homorhythmic**.

Chord progression. See **progression**.

Chromatic. Notes that don't belong to the current key. The opposite of **diatonic**.

Circle of 5ths. A series (or **progression**) of chords whose **roots** are each a 5th lower than the previous chord (e.g. E–A–D–G–C). In practice the bass usually alternates between falling a 5th and rising a 4th, which produces a less angular line from the same set of pitches.

Classical. **1**. In music, the period between about 1750 and 1825. **2**. In a wider sense, any type of music that is regarded as 'art music' rather than pop, folk or jazz – so styles as varied as **Baroque**, **Romantic** and postmodernist can all be described in a very general way as 'classical'.

Close harmony. A style of singing in which most of the accompanying voice parts lie close to the melody and close to each other, often no more than an octave apart.

Closing section. See **codetta**.

Cluster. A dissonant chord that includes several adjacent notes only one step apart from each other.

Coda. A closing section at the end of a movement, song or other piece. Often called an **outro** in pop and rock music.

Codetta. A short **coda**, used to end a section within a longer movement. Also known as a closing section.

Colla voce. Italian for 'with the voice', indicating that an accompaniment should follow the rhythm of the singers.

Coloratura. Elaborate decoration, especially in vocal music, generally employed to display the skill of the singer.

Compass. See **range**.

Compound time. In compound time, the beat is a dotted note that can be divided into three shorter notes of equal length. Time signatures with 6, 9 or 12 as the upper number indicate compound time (e.g. $\frac{6}{8}$, $\frac{6}{4}$, $\frac{9}{8}$, $\frac{12}{8}$). See also **Simple time** and **Metre**.

Concept album. A collection of pop songs related by lyrics that share a common theme.

Concertino. The group of soloists, as opposed to the **ripieno** (the orchestra), in a **concerto grosso**.

Concerto. A large-scale composition for orchestra with a soloist or group of soloists, often in three movements. A **solo concerto** has one soloist, a **concerto grosso** (a genre of the **Baroque** period) has a group of soloists. See also **concertino** and **ripieno**.

Conjunct. A melody that moves mainly by **step** between adjacent notes (the opposite of a **disjunct** melody). Conjunct movement can instead be described as stepwise movement.

Continuo. A bass part (**basso continuo**) in **Baroque** music played by one or more bass instruments (such as cello, bass and bassoon) and used by the players of chordal instruments (such as lute, harpsichord and organ) as the basis from which to fill out the harmonies of the music, sometimes aided by a **figured bass**. The group of instruments that play this part is also known as the continuo.

Contrapuntal. Music in which two or more melodic lines occur simultaneously (a texture known as **counterpoint**).

Contrary motion. Simultaneous melodic lines whose pitches move in opposite directions.

Counterpoint. A texture in which two or more melodic lines occur simultaneously. This texture can also be described as **polyphony**. See also **contrapuntal**.

Countertenor. An adult male voice with a range similar to that of an alto. Today many countertenors use **falsetto** in their higher register.

Cross rhythm. **1**. A rhythm that conflicts with the regular pattern of beats. **2**. The combination of two conflicting rhythms within a single beat (e.g. a triplet of quavers against two normal quavers).

Cue. An individual piece of music in a film score.

Da capo form. A type of **ternary form** (ABA structure) in which the repeat of the A section is indicated by the instruction Da capo ('from the start') instead of being written out. See also **Dal segno**.

Dal segno. Literally 'from the sign'. An instruction to repeat from the bar marked 𝄋.

Development. The central section of **sonata form**. Also used more generally to describe the manipulation and transformation of motifs and themes in any sort of music.

Dialogue. A texture in which motifs are exchanged between different parts without the use of **imitation**.

Diatonic. Notes that belong to the current key. The opposite of **chromatic**.

Diegetic music. In film music, music that occurs as part of the action in the film, such as when a character turns on the radio. Also called 'source music'.

Diminish. **1**. A proportionate decrease in note lengths, e.g. when a rhythm of two crotchets and a minim is diminished it becomes two quavers and a crotchet. **2**. A diminished interval is a semitone smaller than a minor or a perfect interval. Diminution is the opposite of **augmentation**.

Diminished 7th. **1**. An interval notated as a 7th that is one semitone smaller than a minor 7th, such as E to D♭. **2**. A chord based on this interval, and made up of superimposed minor 3rds (or their enharmonic equivalents), for example E–G–B♭–D♭.

Disjunct. A melody that moves mainly in leaps between adjacent notes; the opposite of **conjunct**.

Dissonant. Music whose notes mainly seem to clash harshly when sounded together.

Distortion. An effect that can make the sound of an electric guitar harsher and more gritty.

Djembe. A goblet-shaped drum from West Africa, played with the hands.

Dominant. The fifth note of a major or minor scale (e.g. G is the dominant of C major). A triad on the dominant can be described with the Roman numeral V.

Dominant preparation. A passage that creates expectation for the return of the tonic key, typically at the end of the development in a sonata form movement, by extended use of dominant harmony and by chords that lean onto the dominant. There is also often a dominant pedal.

Dominant 7th chord. A triad on the dominant plus a diatonic 7th above its root. In the key of C the dominant chord is G–B–D and the dominant 7th chord is G–B–D–F.

Dotted rhythms. Successive pairs of notes in which the first is a dotted note and the second is a short note, the two together making a complete beat or complete division of a beat.

Double stopping. Playing two notes at the same time on a string instrument such as the violin.

Double tracking. A recording technique in which a performer sings or plays along with their own prerecorded performance in order to produce a thicker sound.

Doubling. **1**. The performance of the same melody, in unison or in octaves, by two or more musicians at the same time. **2**. Playing two different instruments in a work such as a musical. For example, a saxophone player may be required to double on the flute in some sections.

Drone. The term preferred in folk music for a continuous **pedal** note.

Drum kit. A set of percussion instruments played by one person in a rock group. Usually includes a bass drum (played with a foot-operated beater), hi-hat cymbals (also played with a foot pedal), a snare drum, a suspended cymbal, and one or more tom-toms.

Dynamics. The levels of loudness or softness in music and the symbols used to indicate those levels, such as ***f*** (loud) and ***p*** (soft).

Effects. Methods of modifying sounds through the use of music technology. See **overdrive** and **reverb**.

End title. In film music, the music heard during the 'end credits' (or 'end crawl') of a film.

Enharmonic. Notes or keys that sound the same but are notated differently, such as C♯ and D♭.

Ensemble. A small group of musicians who perform together.

Episode. A passage of music linking two appearances of the same or similar material. See **Ritornello form**.

Exposition. The first section of a **fugue**; the first section of a movement in **sonata form**.

Extended chords. Chords in which further notes a 3rd apart are added to 7th chords to produce chords of the 9th, 11th and 13th above the **root**.

False relation. The effect produced when the natural and chromatically altered versions of a note (such as G and G♯) in different parts occur either simultaneously or in close proximity.

Falsetto. A technique of singing notes higher than the normal top register by using only the edges of the vocal cords.

Fanfare. A short and lively flourish for trumpets or a group of brass instruments, typically used to introduce something or someone.

Figured bass. A **basso continuo** part with figures and other symbols beneath the notes to indicate the harmonies of the music. See also **realisation**.

Fill. In pop music and jazz, a brief improvised flourish (often on drums) to fill the gap between the end of one phrase and the beginning of the next.

Film score. The complete set of original music to accompany a film.

Finale. **1**. The last movement of a multi-movement work such as a **concerto**. **2**. The closing scene in an act of an **opera** or **musical**.

Form. The structure of a musical composition, often symbolised by capital letters. For example, an ABA structure (known as **ternary form**) has three sections, the outer of which (A) contrast with the middle section (B).

Free time. Music in which the rhythm does not have to fit a regular pulse.

Fugato. A passage of music like the opening section of a **fugue**.

Fugue. A **contrapuntal** piece or texture that begins with a single voice (vocal or instrumental) announcing an unaccompanied tune called the subject. Other voices enter with the subject, one at a time and sometimes at different pitches, while the previous voices continue. There is no set structure after this opening section, called the **exposition**, although the voices continue to interweave material (mainly from the subject), using much **imitation** and passing through related keys before the fugue ends in the tonic key. At some point there is often a **stretto** (a 'tightening') where the voices enter in turn with the subject but at closer time intervals than before.

Full score. A score showing the individual parts for all the instruments required. See **short score**.

Genre (pronounced *jon-ruh*). A type of music, such as the concerto, sonata or pop ballad.

Gigue. A fast dance in compound time (or based on triplet rhythms in simple time). Developed from the jig, it was often used as the last movement of a **suite** in the **Baroque** period.

Glissando. A slide from one pitch to another. Sometimes a distinction is made between glissando and **portamento**, although the two terms are now often used interchangeably.

Ground bass. Also called a ground. A bass **ostinato** or constantly repeating bass pattern above which a melody unfolds. A popular genre of the early- and mid-Baroque period.

Harmonic. On string instruments (including the harp and guitar), a very high and pure sound produced by placing a finger on a string very lightly before plucking or bowing.

Harmonic pace. The rate at which chords change. Also known as harmonic rhythm. This could be on every beat, every other beat, every bar, every two bars – there are many possibilities and often the harmonic pace varies throughout a piece.

Harmonic sequence. See **sequence**.

Harmony. The sound produced by a **chord** or succession of chords.

Homophonic. A texture in which one part (usually the highest) has the melodic interest, which the others accompany. If all the parts have the same rhythm, the texture can be described as **chordal** or **homorhythmic**, but if the accompaniment is rhythmically independent of the melody, the texture is described as **melody-and-accompaniment**.

Homorhythmic. A type of **homophonic** texture in which all parts have the same rhythm.

Hurdy Gurdy. An instrument with strings that are set into vibration by the action of a hand-cranked wheel. Some strings are stopped by small wooden levers to produce tunes while others sound as **drones**.

Imitation. A contrapuntal device in which a melody in one part is copied a few notes later in a different part (often at a different pitch) while the melody in the first part continues. If parts exchange ideas without any overlap, the texture is described as **dialogue**, not imitation. See also **canon**.

Imperfect cadence. Almost any chord followed by chord V (the **dominant** chord) at the end of a phrase, having a more unfinished effect than a **perfect cadence**.

Incidental music. Music intended to be performed as part of a play.

Inner pedal. A **pedal** that occurs in the middle of a musical texture rather than in the bass or top part.

Intro. Abbreviation of introduction. As an abbreviation it generally refers to the opening bars of a pop song played before the voice enters.

Instrumental. **1**. Music performed by instruments, without the use of voices. **2**. A section in a pop song that features an instrumental solo, often replacing (but based on the chords of) a sung verse.

Instrumentation. The instruments and voices employed in a piece of music. The term is often used interchangeably with orchestration, which refers to the way that these resources are used.

Interrupted cadence. Chord $V^{(7)}$ followed by any chord except I at the end of a phrase. Usually sounding surprising, as if a perfect cadence has literally been interrupted.

Interval. The distance between two pitches, including both of the pitches that form the interval. So, in the scale of C major, the interval between the first and second notes is a 2nd (C–D), the interval between the first and third notes is a 3rd (C–D–E), and so on.

Inverted pedal. A **pedal** that occurs in the topmost part of a musical texture rather than in the bass or in a middle part.

Key. The scale on which a passage of music is mainly based. The key is named after the home note (**key note**) of the major or minor scale concerned. If a passage is based mainly on notes of the scale of C major, with C as the home note, it is said to be in C major.

Key note. The first (and last) note of a major or minor scale, also known as the tonic and sounding like the home note of the key and the scale.

Kora. A long-necked harp, shaped like a lute, used in West African music.

Layered texture. A texture in which different levels of repeating patterns, each with a distinctive character, are placed on top of one another. Entire layers drop in or out to provide contrasts.

Lead guitar. The part that has, along with the **lead vocal**, the main melodic role in a rock band.

Lead vocal. The part for the main solo singer in a rock band. See also **backing vocals**.

Leap. An interval greater than a **tone** between adjacent notes. The opposite of a **step**. A melody that moves in leaps is said to be **disjunct**.

Leitmotif. A musical idea that is associated with a person, object, place or emotion in a music drama.

Libretto. A document containing all the words of an **opera** or **stage musical**.

Loop. A short section of music that is continually repeated using technology.

Low whistle. A recorder-like instrument used in Irish traditional music. It is longer and deeper in range than the smaller and more familiar tin whistle.

Lyrics. The words of a pop song or of the songs in a musical.

Main title. In film music, the music heard during the 'opening credits' (or 'opening crawl') of a film.

Melismatic. A style **word setting** in which several notes are sung to the same syllable. The opposite of **syllabic**.

Melodic sequence. See **sequence**.

Melody. A musically satisfying series of single notes, often described as a tune.

Melody-and-accompaniment. A **homophonic** texture in which the accompaniment has some degree of rhythmic independence from the melody.

Metre or **meter**. The repeating patterns of strong and weak beats that underpin the rhythms of many types of music. Duple metre has two beats per bar (strong–weak), triple metre has three (strong–weak–weak) and quadruple metre has four (strong–weak–weak–weak). See also **Simple time** and **Compound time**.

Mezzo soprano. A female singing voice, lower than soprano but higher than alto.

Middle eight. See **bridge**.

Mode. A scale of seven pitches. Major and minor scales are types of modes, but the term is usually reserved for other types of scales, such as the **Aeolian mode**. Music that uses a mode is described as modal music.

Modulation. A change of key.

Monophonic. A texture consisting of an unaccompanied melody, performed either by a soloist or by many people in unison or in octaves.

Monotone. Single pitch. Singing on a monotone means chanting on one note, without varying the pitch.

Mordent. An **ornament** played as a rapid wiggle from the printed note to the note above and back (upper mordent, written 𝆗) or to the note below and back (lower mordent, written 𝆘).

Motif. A short, distinctive melody or rhythm used in various ways to form much longer passages of music.

Movement. An independent section in a longer piece of music.

Multi-tracking. A process commonly used in pop music in which individual tracks of sound from one or more performers are recorded independently and then played back together.

Murky bass. An 18th-century term for broken octaves (rapidly alternating notes that are an octave apart)

Musical. A large-scale piece of music theatre, incorporating acting and singing to an instrumental accompaniment, and usually including spoken dialogue and dance. See also **book**, **finale (2)**, **libretto**, **opera** and **numbers**.

Mute. A device to alter the sound of an instrument, most commonly used by players of brass and string instrument. *Con sordino* means 'with mute', *senza sordino* means without mute.

Natural trumpet. A trumpet without valves, in common use before about 1825.

Numbers. The individual musical items in a stage musical (e.g. songs, choruses and dances).

Obbligato aria. An **aria**, generally from the Baroque period, which includes a part for a solo instrument that is almost as important as the vocal part.

Octave. The distance between a note and the nearest note with the same letter name, for example from C to the C seven steps higher.

Opera. A large-scale composition for the theatre, involving staged drama sung to an instrumental accompaniment. **Operetta** is shorter, lighter and typically includes spoken dialogue. See also **musical**.

Oratorio. A large-scale composition for solo voices, choir and orchestra, usually on a Biblical subject, but intended for concert performance.

Orchestration. The process of arranging music for orchestral instruments, having regard to balance, colour and texture. The term is often used interchangeably with instrumentation, which more strictly means the list of instruments (and voices) used in a piece.

Ornaments. Notes, often indicated by special signs, that decorate the main notes of a melody. See **acciaccatura**, **appoggiatura**, **mordent**, **slide**, **trill**.

Ostinato. A rhythmic, melodic or harmonic pattern repeated many times in succession. Often called a **riff** in jazz, pop and rock. See also **ground bass**.

Outro. See **coda**.

Overdub. The process of adding additional sound tracks to an existing recording.

Overdrive. A guitar effect that produces a deliberately distorted sound.

Pan. A control that determines the position (from left to right) of a sound in a stereo field.

Parallel harmonies. A succession of similar chords whose notes all move in the same direction.

Passing notes. Non-chord notes that move by step between the notes of adjacent chords.

Pedal. **1**. A sustained or repeated note, often the **tonic** or **dominant** and most commonly in the bass, sounded against changing harmonies. Also called a pedal point and known as a **drone** in folk music. See also **inner pedal** and **inverted pedal**. **2**. A foot-operated lever on instruments such as the piano, organ and harp.

Pentatonic scale. A scale of five pitches to the octave. Pitches 1, 2, 3, 5 and 6 from a major scale form a **pentatonic major** while pitches 1, 3, 4, 5, and 7 from a natural minor scale form a **pentatonic minor**.

Perfect cadence. Chord $V^{(7)}$ followed by chord I (the **tonic** chord) at the end of a phrase, tending to have a more conclusive effect than an **imperfect cadence**.

Periodic phrasing. Paired phrases of similar length that sound like a question followed by an answer. Sometimes called 'balanced phrasing', it is a typical feature of music in the Classical period.

Phase shifter. An electronic process that can add a 'sweeping effect' to a sound.

Phrase. A section of melody that makes a statement, although not necessarily a complete statement, and that often ends with a **cadence**.

Plagal cadence. Chord IV followed by chord I (the **tonic** chord) at the end of a phrase, having a conclusive effect rather like a sung 'amen'.

Polyphony. A texture in which two or more melodic lines occur simultaneously. This texture can also be described as **counterpoint**.

Polyrhythmic. A texture of conflicting rhythms played together.

Portamento. A continuous glide in pitch between two notes, more subtle than **glissando**.

Pre-chorus. A short section at the end of the verse in a pop song, designed to propel the music into the actual chorus.

Progression. A succession of two or more chords, also known as a chord progression or harmonic progression. Sometimes incorrectly described as a chord sequence (the term **sequence** has a different meaning). See **circle of 5ths**.

Push. A type of **syncopation** used in pop and jazz in which notes are played ('pushed') slightly ahead of the beat.

Quartal harmony. Chords based on intervals of a 4th rather than the more usual 3rds.

Range. A span of pitches from low to high that a voice or instrument can produce, or that is found in a passage of music. Also known as the compass.

Realisation. The process or result of adding chords and decoration to a **figured bass**.

Recitative. Vocal music that mimics the rhythms of ordinary speech.

Register. A particular part of the **range** of a voice or instrument, such as a high register or a low register. Similar in meaning to **tessitura**.

Related keys. Keys whose scales have most of their notes in common. For example, C major and G major are closely related because all their notes are the same except that C major has F whereas G major has F♯.

Reverb. Abbreviation of reverberation. The reflections that occur when sound is made in an enclosed space. Digitally produced reverb is often added to recordings.

Rhythm. The patterns produced by notes and rests of various lengths.

Rhythm guitar. The part that primarily supplies the harmony in a rock band.

Riff. In jazz, pop and rock, a short melodic pattern repeated many times in succession. See also **Ostinato**.

Ripieno. The orchestra, as distinct from the **concertino** (the soloists), in a **concerto grosso**.

Ritornello form. A structure used for longer movements in the **Baroque** period that begins with a section in the tonic key. Parts of this music then return in related keys, separated by modulating **episodes** for one or more soloists. A final ritornello re-establishes the tonic key. Ritornello is Italian for a little return and refers to the opening section usually being shortened when it returns.

Romantic. The predominant musical style in the 19th century.

Rondo form. A musical structure in which a main section (called the rondo theme) alternates with contrasting **episodes**, creating a pattern such as ABACA.

Root. The note that corresponds with the letter-name of a chord. For example, the root of a chord of C major is always the note C, no matter which of its three pitches (C, E or G) is the bass note.

Rubato. Tiny fluctuations in **tempo** for expressive effect.

Samba. A dance and highly syncopated type of music from Brazil. A stylised form of the dance is popular as a type of ballroom dancing.

Sample. A short segment taken from an existing recording for reuse in a new piece.

Scale. A set of notes that go up or down in order.

Scalic. Related to a musical scale.

Scena. In music theatre, a continuous piece of vocal music comprising several distinct sections.

Semitone. Half of a **tone**: the smallest **interval** in common use in western music.

Sequence. The immediate repetition at a different pitch of a melody (melodic sequence) or chord progression (harmonic sequence).

Short score. A reduction of a work for many instruments onto just a few staves. See **full score**.

Shuffle rhythm. In jazz and some types of pop music, the division of the beat into pairs of notes in which the first is a little longer than the second. Also known as **swing rhythm** or **swing quavers**.

Simple time. In simple time, the beat is a note that can be divided into two shorter notes of equal length. Time signatures with 2, 3 or 4 as the upper number indicate simple time (e.g. $\frac{2}{4}$, $\frac{2}{2}$, $\frac{3}{4}$, $\frac{3}{8}$, $\frac{4}{4}$). See also **Compound time** and **Metre**.

Slide. An ornament common in the Baroque period, consisting of two notes that rapidly rise by step to the main note. The notes of the ornament are printed in small type.

Sonata. In the Classical period and later, a work in three or four movements for either piano alone or for a solo instrument (such as a flute or violin) with piano.

Sonata form. The most common structure for the first movement (and often other movements) of sonatas, symphonies and other types of music in the Classical period and later. The main ideas are presented in the tonic (the first **subject**) and in a contrasting but related key (the second **subject**) in an opening section called the **exposition**, which usually ends with a **codetta**. These ideas are then extended in a central section (the **development**), which is followed by a final section (the **recapitulation**) in which both first and second subjects normally return in the tonic key. The structure ends with a final section called the **coda**, designed to assert the tonic key.

Sonority. The character of musical sounds either individually or in combination. See also **timbre**.

Soprano. The highest female singing voice.

Stab. A term used in pop and jazz for a loud, detached chord, often played by brass or full orchestra.

Step. An interval of a **tone** or **semitone** between adjacent notes. The opposite of a **leap**. A melody that moves in steps is said to have stepwise or **conjunct** motion.)

Stretto. A section of a **fugue** in which entries of the **subject** occur closer together than previously so that they overlap more tightly.

Strophic form. A structure found mainly in simple songs in which the same music is used for each of several verses. The form can be expressed as AAA... etc.

Structure. See **form**.

Subject. The **theme** of a **fugue** or one of two important themes in **sonata form**.

Suite. A collection of pieces (often dances) intended to be performed together.

Sus chord. In pop and jazz, a chord containing a 4th or 2nd instead of a 3rd above the root (sounding like the **dissonance** heard in a **suspension**).

Suspension. An effect that occurs when a note from one chord is held over to (or repeated in) a chord to which it does not belong. This creates a momentary expressive **dissonance** that is resolved (i.e. it ends) when the dissonant note then moves to a chord note. See also **sus chord**.

Swing quavers, **swing rhythm**. See **shuffle rhythm**.

Syllabic. A style **word setting** in which in which each syllable is set to its own note. The opposite of **melismatic**.

Syncopation. Strongly accented notes played off or against the beat.

Talking drum. An African drum with various local names, almost always in an hour-glass shape and played with a hooked beater. It has considerable tonal variety depending on where it is struck and how the tension on the drum head is varied, making it possible to mimic the patterns of speech.

Tasto solo. A passage in a **continuo** part where no chords are required.

Tempo. The speed at which music is performed.

Tenor. The highest male singing voice, apart from **countertenor**.

Ternary form. A three-part structure in which the first and last sections are similar while the central section creates a contrast (often summarized as ABA form). See also **Da capo form**.

Terraced dynamics. Clear contrasts between loud and soft sections rather than gradual changes. Terraced dynamics are a feature of much **Baroque** music.

Tessitura. The average **range** of a passage. Similar in meaning to **register** but generally used for vocal rather than instrumental music.

Texture. The relationship between the simultaneous layers in a passage of music.

Theme. A musical idea (usually a melody) that plays an important role in a piece of music.

Tierce de Picardie. A major tonic chord ending a cadence in a minor key.

Timbre. (pronounced *tam-bruh*). Tone colour. The clarinet has a different timbre to the trumpet, but the clarinet also has different timbres in various parts of its **range**. Timbre can also be affected by the way an instrument is played, for example by using a **mute** or plucking a string instead of using the bow. See also **sonority**.

Title hook. A short and catchy **motif** set to the words of the title of a pop song.

Tonality. The use of major and/or minor keys in music, and their relationship. Music that uses major and minor keys is called tonal music. For exam purposes, tonality also includes **modal** and **atonal** music.

Tone. **1**. An interval of two **semitones**, for example C–D. **2**. The **timbre** of a particular instrument or voice.

Tonic. The first (and last) note of a major or minor scale, also known as the key note. A triad on the tonic can be described with the Roman numeral I.

Transcription. A score made from a recording. Also used to refer to an arrangement.

Transpose. The process of writing or performing music at a higher or lower pitch.

Tremolo. The continuous, rapid repetition of either a single pitch or two alternating pitches.

Triad. A chord of three pitches consisting of a bass note and the notes a 3rd and a 5th above it.

Triadic. Related to a **triad**.

Trill. An ornament (often shown as ***tr***) consisting of the rapid repeated alternation of two pitches a step apart.

Triplet. Three notes played in the time taken by two of the same value.

Truck driver's gear change. A nickname for the jerky effect caused by modulating up a semitone to repeat a verse or a chorus in a pop song.

Tutti. Everyone. A passage in which all or most members of an ensemble are playing.

Uilleann pipes. A type of Irish bagpipe used in many kinds of folk music. The air supply comes from elbow-operated bellows. The range of notes is wider than the more familiar Great Highland bagpipes of Scotland, and the tone is sweeter.

Underscore. Background or non-**diegetic** film music. Music played under spoken dialogue.

Unison. The effect of two or more people performing the same note(s).

Verse and chorus form. A song structure common in pop and rock. Each verse, which has different words but the same music, is followed by a contrasting chorus in which both words and music are the same on every appearance. The song may start with an **intro** and end with an **outro**. The structure may also include a **pre-chorus**, a contrasting **bridge** and/or **instrumental (2)**.

Vibrato. Small, rapid fluctuations in pitch used to give warmth and expression to a note.

Violone. A bowed bass string instrument that sometimes has frets (like a guitar) and that is a predecessor of the double bass. See also **Bass viol**.

Virtuoso. A performer of outstanding technical ability. Music written for such a performer is described as virtuosic and demonstrates a performer's virtuosity.

Vocables. Nonsense syllables in a song (e.g. 'doo doo doo').

Vocal music. Music intended to be sung.

Wah-wah. A guitar effect or brass mute that can mimic the human voice saying 'wah-wah'.

Walking bass. A bass line that creates a steady tread by moving mainly in identical note lengths (crotchets or quavers) in contrast to the movement of the upper parts

Word painting. The illustration in music of the meaning or suggestion of particular words or phrases in a text, such as the use of a discord for the word 'pain'.

Word setting. The way in which notes are allocated to the syllables of the text in **vocal music**. The style of setting may be **syllabic**, **melismatic** or a combination of both, and it may include examples of **word painting**.

Acknowledgements:

Rhinegold Education is grateful to the following publishers for permission to use printed excerpts in its publications:

'Defying Gravity' (from The Broadway Musical *Wicked*): Words & Music by Stephen Schwartz,
© Copyright 2003 Greydog Music, Rodgers & Hammerstein Theatrical Europe Limited.
All Rights Reserved. International Copyright Secured.

'Killer Queen': Words & Music by Freddie Mercury,
© Copyright 1974 Queen Music Limited,
EMI Music Publishing Limited.
All Rights Reserved. International Copyright Secured.

'Samba Em Prelúdio': Words by Vinicius De Moraes,
Music by Baden Powell & Vinicius De Moraes,
© Copyright 1962 Universal Music Publishing S L,
Universal Music Publishing MGB Limited/
Tonos Musikverlags Gmbh.
All Rights Reserved. International Copyright Secured.

Star Wars (Main Theme): Music by John Williams,
© Copyright 1977 Bantha Music, USA, Warner/
Chappell Music Limited.
All Rights Reserved. International Copyright Secured.

Picture credit:

Page 28: courtesy Nicolas Collins